"I cannot recommend this book highly enough for anyone who feels even slightly weighed down by the pressures of modern life—our jobs, families, schedules, and unrealized dreams. Margaret's inspired message will force you to ask relevant questions about your own life—questions that perhaps God has been waiting to hear."

— TONY GUERRERO, director of creative arts, Saddleback Church; recording artist/composer/producer

"I have never read a book that spoke so deeply to my soul as *Coming Up for Air*. It is one of the most authentic and inspiring looks at life. Anyone needing to slow down and understand how to live life in the moment should read this book. It indeed is a breath of fresh air!"

— BRENDA COMBS, producer, neighborhood ministry, Willow Creek Community Church

"*Coming Up for Air* is an intimate account of how to take time out from the life you create for yourself and return to the life God really wants for you. Margaret has a beautiful way of taking you along on her journey and allowing her thoughts and prayers to sink into your own reality. You'll be empowered by the ride."

— BONNIE PRITCHARD, executive producer of *Songs 4 Worship*

"With disarming humor and compelling candor, this book dares you to look boldly at your personal journey, get your bearings, and revive a passion for living."

— MICHAEL NOLAN, author, scriptwriter, and journalist

"Becker plunges into murky water and floats to the surface spiritually refreshed. Her smart and sassy sense of humor will make you wonder if she missed her calling as a stand-up comedian. Her journey of self-discovery reminds us to live in the moment—in the presence of God—bathing in the beauty of His awesome masterpiece."

— TINA CERNERO, vice president, creative services, BMG Columbia House, Inc.

"*Coming Up for Air* is so relatable, so real, so filled with visual representations of life's little epiphanies that it grabbed my hand and became my journey, spawning a driven determination within my soul to employ the principles Margaret brings to life. She beckons positive spiritual, personal, and emotional growth from within you simply by telling her own story. Kind of reminds me of Someone else I know."

— KAT DAVIS, author of thedailyverse.com; relationship marketing manager, EMI Christian Music Group

Simple Acts to Redefine Your Life

Margaret.Becker
coming up for air

NAVPRESS®

BRINGING TRUTH TO LIFE

OUR GUARANTEE TO YOU

We believe so strongly in the message of our books that we
are making this quality guarantee to you. If for any reason
you are disappointed with the content of this book, return
the title page to us with your name and address and we will
refund to you the list price of the book. To help us serve you
better, please briefly describe why you were disappointed.
Mail your refund request to: NavPress, P.O. Box 35002,
Colorado Springs, CO 80935.

The Navigators is an international Christian organization. Our mission is to reach, disciple, and equip people to know Christ and to make Him known through successive generations. We envision multitudes of diverse people in the United States and every other nation who have a passionate love for Christ, live a lifestyle of sharing Christ's love, and multiply spiritual laborers among those without Christ.

NavPress is the publishing ministry of The Navigators. NavPress publications help believers learn biblical truth and apply what they learn to their lives and ministries. Our mission is to stimulate spiritual formation among our readers.

ISBN 1-57683-934-6

Cover design by Charles Brock, The Design Works Group
Cover photo by Getty Images
Creative Team: Terry Behimer, Arvid Wallen, Traci Mullins, Cara Iverson, Angie Messinger

Some of the anecdotal illustrations in this book are true to life and are included with the permission of the persons involved. All other illustrations are composites of real situations, and any resemblance to people living or dead is coincidental.

Published in association with the literary agency of Alive Communications, Inc., 7680 Goddard Street, Suite 200, Colorado Springs, Colorado 80920 (www.alivecommunications.com).

Unless otherwise identified, all Scripture quotations in this publication are taken from the HOLY BIBLE: NEW INTERNATIONAL VERSION® (NIV®). Copyright © 1973, 1978, 1984 by International Bible Society. Used by permission of Zondervan Publishing House. All rights reserved. Other versions used include: the *King James Version* (KJV); and the *Holman Christian Standard Bible*® (HCSB). All rights reserved.

Becker, Margaret, 1959-
    Coming up for air : simple acts to redefine your life / Margaret Becker.
        p. cm.
    Includes bibliographical references.
    ISBN 1-57683-934-6
    1. Becker, Margaret, 1959- 2. Christian biography—United States. 3. Gospel musicians—United States—
Biography. I. Title.
    BR1725.B413A3 2006
    277.3'083092—dc22

                                                                                            2005030696

Printed in the United States of America

1 2 3 4 5 6 / 10 09 08 07 06

FOR A FREE CATALOG OF NAVPRESS BOOKS & BIBLE STUDIES,
CALL 1-800-366-7788 (USA) OR 1-800-839-4769 (CANADA)

To my parents, Phil and Peg Becker

• • •

Contents

Part Three: Breathing Free

Holding My Breath

*You must be the change you
wish to see in the world.*

—Gandhi

A while back, I had a life-disconnect.
I don't know what triggered it. It wasn't major regret or terrible crisis. I had achieved many of my dreams, and I loved what my hands had found to do. All I know is that something just didn't feel right about it all. From time to time, I felt my life separate from me as though it belonged to someone else. It was as if I were fulfilling a role that was familiar but, in truth, was not my own.

It wasn't always that way. What began as an uphill trek with me at the front of my life, guiding and pulling where I wanted, somewhere along the way became inverted. The momentum of my journey overtook me, and when I came to, I was no longer leading—I was running to catch up.

What ensued was a series of awakenings more than anything else—a series of small discoveries that left me with questions and feelings of greater realities that seemed just beyond my grasp. I was alone there in this "in between." I was touching but not feeling, breathing but not refreshed. I was moving through life like an alien visitor, insulated in a bubble—a sensory buffer that left me feeling removed.

Mind you, it wasn't like that every day but just enough to signal that I was losing touch with my own life. The daily routine that should have felt comforting seemed confining, mundane, and, I guess—with some deep-seated remnant of a Baby Boomer work ethic—too easy. And so as it is with me and these things, I took drastic measures.

As I look back now, I'm just thankful that I didn't choose to cut off my hair and revise my first name to something confusing ending with a vowel, like "Maggeii." Instead, I opted to regroup and assess my life.

What follows is an account of what that regrouping was like. It's messy. It's funny. It's tragic and true. Some of what you read will be in journal form and some in just plain story form, because just like life, it has all come to me in misshapen, untamed spurts that resist structure. These thoughts and experiences inevitably wound up archived in my brain, or on napkins and boarding passes, or in old folders on my computer with detailed file names like "stuff" and "more stuff."

And that is just how my life has been: anything but orderly. This whole journey has been an evolution of learning more than it's been a time line. This is how my soul "came to." This is how my eyes were opened. This is how I have meandered through words, not always able to reach a point.

Part One

Breathing In

*What lies behind us and what lies before us are
tiny matters compared to what lies within us.*
—RALPH WALDO EMERSON

Chapter One

Breaking the Surface

December 1995. I thought I was just taking a long vacation, four weeks to be exact. I needed it.

This vacation was going to be unlike any other I'd ever known. I was going to unplug entirely and do absolutely nothing. No phone calls. No faxes. No check-ins to the office. No long overdue work related projects. No catching up on correspondence. No self-help makeovers. Just *nothing*. Wide-open calendar space. Nothing written in the whole month. A time to be indulgent. Sleep till noon. Play Solitaire with *real* playing cards. Watch endless reruns of *Columbo*. Eat chocolate for breakfast. *That* kind of vacation.

I was used to traveling. I'm a singer, or a writer, or a speaker— depending on whom you ask. In fact, I never know what to write on forms that ask for my occupation, because what I do has felt like pleasure and play for most of my life. It's a living by default. Most of the time, I feel guilty listing it as "work."

The worst I can say about my career over the past two decades is that the travel gets old. Packing and unpacking take it right out of me. Who would've thought that finding the correct underwear and shirt could be such a mental drain or that sitting motionless for hours mesmerized by the din of jet engines could be such a chore?

But even on the worst days, with delays, close-connection "travel sweat," hunger pangs, and middle seats, it sure beats bill collecting at Sears. And this is my mantra as I run thirteen gates in the Dallas/Fort Worth airport, trying to beat my best time of four minutes.

With each step I remember the "Rs": Reilly, Restuchia, Richards, Richenstein, Romano, Ruggiero. The names of people that I was responsible to "shake down" for Mr. Sears and Roebuck in my first "real job" after college. What a miserable occupation for someone like me. Half the time, I'd take part of my own paycheck and pay on the delinquent accounts. Trying to collect money from people who just don't have any is hard enough, but when you add the duty of talking to a woman about repossessing her washer and dryer or, worse yet, her refrigerator, you're placing your life on the line. I had to do it under an assumed name. It was just too dangerous otherwise.

Seems like it was a million years ago, yet the memory of it is like a growling dog whose breath I feel at my heels, ready to nip if I don't keep moving. And I had spent years doing just that—moving, going, being, fulfilling obligations and dreams, running from the dogs—to the point of exhaustion. Not physical exhaustion. That would be a handy excuse to do what I ended up doing. It's deeper than that, harder to justify to others. Exhaustion somewhere deep inside, the kind that makes a person overly sensitive or never able to catch up in life. It's the kind of fatigue that permeates everything yet leaves no calling card. You can barely explain it because it's everything and nothing all at the same time.

It was sometime earlier in 1995 that I woke up in a hotel room for the hundredth time, again unable to remember where the bathroom was, that I came face-to-face with my exhaustion in a way I couldn't deny. Stumbling first to the closet and then into the faux maple dresser, I fell inelegantly onto the Barcalounger, where I was forced to assess my surroundings. My eyes adjusted slowly in the dark: basic brass floor lamp overhead, coarse, nubby upholstery on the chair, TV bleeding through the wall next door . . . ah, yes, the Comfort Inn.

I sat there for a while, wondering if all frequent travelers have these hotel blackouts. And after a little while, the Barca started to actually feel like a good place to meditate on the current state of my life. When the sleep timer on my neighbor's TV went off, I asked myself the question that any hardworking overachiever hates to ask: *When was the last time I had a vacation?* And the even more frightening, *When was the last time I truly relaxed?*

I had to turn on my computer to find the answer. Consulting the calendar, I scrolled furiously until the tiny little watch icon popped up on the screen, warning me not to push my luck. I went back years. I couldn't find the last time. There was no last time since escaping the growling dog at twenty-five.

Swathed there in the yellow light illuminating from the hotel parking lot, I dreamed the impossible dream: to escape. Escape from my life with no guitars and cords, no oversized baggage, no "work"—just for a while. Escape to a beach, the place that has always held the sights and sounds of freedom for me. When I was a kid growing up on Long Island, summer vacations were always filled with endless days on the Atlantic shore. They had a trance-like effect on reality, blending one day into the other, until school, responsibility, and structure seemed concepts as foreign as taking cod liver oil for all that ails you.

I hatched my plan at the Comfort Inn. By morning, I was on the Internet researching good beach deals. I wanted something cheap, not too hot, right on the water, secluded and clean. I settled on Destin, Florida, next winter, after all the year's obligations were fulfilled.

I needed time. Time alone. Time away. Downtime. Just time.

The following week, I told my record company, my booking

agent, my managers, and my family about my decision. The standard response was, "Is everything okay? Are you in some sort of crisis?" I felt foolish trying to explain it. Why does something have to be desperately wrong before a person is excused from the daily grind?

My answer was disjointed and seemingly deceptive. There was nothing massively wrong. I just felt out of touch with my life, like it was ahead of me, always slightly out of my reach. I was chasing it rather than leading it, and catching up only from time to time. I'd almost wished I had a big crash or crisis on which to blame my need to retreat, because with each subsequent explanation, the whole thing sounded more and more self-indulgent. But in my heart, I knew that it wasn't. I feared that if I didn't make the time to "get off the merry-go-round," I might blink my eyes and be another ten years down the road. I needed this, for reasons not even I fully understood.

So December came and I packed for my winter beach retreat. I took the haphazard approach. I scooped up a stack of soft T-shirts, sweats, worn-out jeans, and all the saggy socks you can't ever wear in public. I did it like they do in the movies: in a rush. I packed like that without looking back. I didn't want to think. I had to just keep moving. *Must get to Gulf. Must put feet in sand. Must . . .*

The escape commenced. It felt reckless, sloppy, loose, and so much unlike my life as I had come to know it. When I crossed the Alabama line from Tennessee, I forced myself to turn off my cell phone. It was my next act of defiance and bravery. The world would go on without me, and when I rejoined it, I planned to enter more peacefully. How? I wasn't sure, but I'd give it my best shot.

It was in Florala, Alabama, that "Jimmy Crack Corn" started playing over and over in my head for reasons I don't *ever* want to understand. *No big deal,* I told myself as I turned on the radio in an attempt to drown the song out. *I am a successful, well-adjusted woman. I'm just a little tired,* I reasoned. *I'm still sane—I think.*

This is how it all started.

Chapter Two

Airing Out

It is well after midnight when I arrive at the Howard. I take my time driving from the Realtor's after-hours lockbox to the rental property. As far as directions are concerned, all that I have to go on is the brochure I've received in the mail showing the front of the house obscured by thick green beach brush. I'm not sure I'd recognize the house even in daylight, but like a mirage coming to life, it finally emerges at the end of a quiet cul-de-sac, its warm porch light cooing to me.

I come to a stop in the tiny driveway, cracking open the car door to the smell of salt and the sound of crashing waves. Before stepping out, I let my forehead rest on the steering wheel for a moment. I know I have been led here. I feel it in my soul. With a heavy sigh of relief, I whisper, "Thank You, thank You, thank You."

Grabbing the lightest bag, I scale the front steps. The Gulf isn't visible, but its presence swirls around me like a friendly tornado. Before me is a thick oak door. Just to the right of the entry, there is a full cord of neatly stacked firewood, a nice offering.

The key slides easily into the lock. I brace myself. This could be really good or *really* bad. My bad hotel experiences have left me scarred for life. I will be spending the next four weeks here. I hope

I'm not afraid to sit on the couch or eat off the plates.

When the door swings open, my fears vanish. Stepping in tentatively, I am pleasantly surprised. It is stunning. The entire back
wall is glass with the moonlit Gulf just beyond its surface, the view
stretched across like the screen of a 3-D movie. It is just as I'd
hoped, only better.

Slowly, I walk into the living room. The space has a wall just big
enough to hold the fireplace, which opens to both the dining room
and living room. Windows frame the sides of each room, and where
they end, white walls begin. Beneath my feet is a rust-colored, polished
cement floor. I plop down in the crisp wicker chair and take it all
in. The décor: elegant West Indies. Dark wood, comfortable. Clean.
Clean. Clean. Best of all, clean.

A basket filled with fresh fruit and flowers sits on the coffee table
with a note that reads, "Enjoy! If you need anything, call us," signed
by the Realtor. I couldn't in my wildest imagination picture myself
"needing" anything more. I was feeling pleasantly piggish as it was.

It takes me less than a half hour to move my meager belongings
into the master bedroom, which also peers out onto the Gulf. Finally
settled into paradise, I climb into the four-poster bed, exhausted. I
feel like I've rolled a boulder up a hill.

As I lie there adjusting to the sounds of the house, focused on
the rhythm of muffled surf just beyond my window, I fall into a
deep sleep. With every crash and retreat, I slip further away until I
remember nothing more, and for the first time in a long time, I sleep
without dreaming.

* * *

I'm not sure what it is about the rhythmic function of water. There
is something inherently universal and eternal in it. It witnesses to
the water in all of us, both "minerally" and spiritually. It is soothing

and reminiscent of things way beyond my control, my imagination, my domain.

My eyes are burning from the cold air as I greet my first morning on the back deck. Over the pale green horizon, I see a tiny glow of pink resting on the edge of the world. It is a hint of what is to come. Bundled up in well-worn sweats (eating pants, as I call them due to their expandable waist), I am trying to feel everything before me while thinking of nothing.

How do you turn off your own brain? I wish I knew a way. Some say there are "arts" and "spiritual practices" that can be employed to "center yourself." Yoga, meditation. The closest I come is prayer. Something about prayer is calming to me. Perhaps it's the thought that there is a force beyond my control that is guiding me, that actually has a handle on all things both great and small. Maybe it's just the discipline of concentrating on something else besides my own steps, my own myopic journey. I think prayer led me here.

It's difficult to understand all of it as I watch the first edge of sun blur the horizon. I am a spiritual being. Of this I am sure. I know it every time I see a spider's web or a newborn baby's fingers, hear a mourning dove cry or the mingled laughter of young children and wise crones. I am convinced the world is not random. There is absolute order here, although I know it is absolutely over my head in theory.

I remember when I first recognized this order, its power and its comfort. It came into focus in the form of phantom monsters in my bedroom dispelled by a prayer. It piqued my curiosity in the twelve stations of the cross hung around the perimeter of our church. The Man, the God, who was both celebrated and betrayed in those paintings, drew me, tugging at my heartstrings with His unselfish suffering and gaining my absolute respect by His unending loyalty to all who harmed Him. All that pain, all that suffering—for me? For my freedom to enter into a relationship with Him? It was a concept that challenged me then, as it does now. My deepest self understood that this being, this Christ, was my ultimate reason to be. It bore witness to the inner workings of my soul.

It was those same inner workings that demanded this retreat. My True North, my center, was getting difficult to see or sense. As a person with an ultimate purpose under an Ultimate Being, I had to adjust. I had to gain a sense of clarity as given through my center, my faith, my Christ. I know enough to know when I am "on track," and I know enough to know when I am "askew." For too long, I have been askew.

So here I am, because I must be. I say my first morning prayer. It is simple and direct: "Lord, You know where I am if You are feeling chatty. Otherwise, I am going to *try* to rest in Your silence. Amen."

• • •

My second morning at the beach is lovely. After a long hot shower in the "House Beautiful" five-by-five shower room, I find the CD player and set "On Earth as It Is in Heaven" and "Gabriel's Oboe" from Ennio Morricone's *The Mission* to play over and over. Opening wide the doors in the living room, I pull up the wicker chair and face it outward. Here I sit in a thick cotton robe, soaking wet, in the nineteen-degree cold. Somewhere in my mind, I hear my father in his New York brogue chiding, "Are you dating a guy from the power company or something? You're letting all the heat out!" Irresponsible usage of the heat pump, yet another perk from paying taxes and getting root canals.

Today the wind is northerly, blowing through the house, rustling magazines and slamming doors. In the distance, I see a heron dive abruptly into the dark green horizon.

This morning I have one droning, freeing thought: *This is life.* As I think it, I become conscious of my own breath, pulling in and expelling, all without my permission. This action takes place count-less times a day—it is necessary for my existence—yet I haven't noted it in years.

For a moment I think I understand how it might feel to have escaped peril through the strength of my own two feet, to have finally found a safe place beyond harm's reach, to know that what was before is no more and what awaits will surely be better.

I am freezing out here, breaking all the rules, but I don't care. The shock of the frigid air begins to stir something to life inside me. I sit until my toes turn numb—thankful for the silence and the sound, thankful for the cold, thankful for the space.

Space—something I haven't had lately. I used to think it was measured in feet and inches. But then somewhere along life's path, I recognized that it is a discipline, a state of mind. You must create it, protect it, and give up things to have it. It means letting yourself say no once in a while. It means carving out time to do nothing on a regular basis. It means making time to air out—finding those ways that your individual soul is fed and intentionally employing them. It means that and so much more that I don't understand right now, as it applies to me and only me. It's part of what I hope to dis-cover over these next few weeks.

．．．

Before I left home in Nashville, I went to an antique store in search of a Christmas present for a friend. On the way out of the shop, I noticed an antique aluminum Christmas tree in the window, com-plete with the color wheel. I recognized the tree immediately as the exact one I enjoyed all throughout my childhood.

As it is every Christmas, I *always* buy myself a gift—one of my guilty pleasures. Seeing how close it was to the twenty-fifth, the owner sold me the entire set—in the original box—for fifty dollars. I stole it.

On this winter morning in Florida, I unpack it with the intention of losing myself in memories of a time when there was nothing but space and possibility. Carefully pulling the plain brown wrapper sleeves off the silver tinsel branches, I begin the familiar pre-setup process of "repair." Some of the tinsel is shimmying up the more damaged branches, so I forage through the drawers in "my" house until I find some Scotch tape. Here I sit, cross-legged on the floor in my favorite sweatshirt and jeans, employing the age-old poor man's repair technique of taping the tinsel at the base.

When I bought the tree, I had a specific moment in mind. It was the moment each year when I would slide underneath our Christmas tree on my back, eyes closed, counting silently. On "three," I'd open them to take in the glittery world above. It always made me feel as though I were somewhere else—somewhere off planet earth. A place where everything is possible and no mystery is fully known. I want to experience that perspective again, from the floor up. I hope it will be the same.

The bottom level of branches has to be off in order for me to fit, and though the tree seems much smaller all these years later, looking up through the silver tinsel splay does not disappoint. It takes my breath away just as it always had. And for a moment, I am six years old and on the verge of the kind of magic that brings undeserved gifts beyond imagining.

This is how I spend most of the day, slowly decorating the antique tree with tiny, brightly colored bulbs, remembering what it felt like to believe in all things.

●　●　●

Since my first day of "detox," I've been doing nothing—at least I've been trying to. "Nothing" is no easy task when you live your life constantly running one hundred miles per hour. I think I have emotional vertigo. Everything is a little off-kilter. All the movements are familiar yet exaggerated. It's similar to the way I feel when I first get off a treadmill. My steps take on some sort of hyper-speed element, and I walk like a cat with a bad case of ear mites. That's how my first few paces toward "nothing" have been. I stagger like a stiff-legged cadaver from a 1950s B movie. With arms flat like paddles outstretched in front of me and a blank stare, I wobble toward "nothing."

Today I feel antsy inside. *Aren't there things to do? Is there something I forgot to tell someone about whatever? Doesn't the kitchen counter need to be wiped down? And what about those plants outside on the deck? Surely they need water.*

Sit still. Enjoy the view. Remember how good it all felt when you first got here? I have to force myself to sit still and watch the Gulf. Looking at the water for hours was all I had dreamed of, yet now it is something I can't do.

My hands clamp around the arms of the weather-worn Adirondack chair. I try to make sense of my hyper energy. Slowing down seems like an ancient art form that I recognize as valuable but whose lines I can't seem to trace with my own hand. It is lovely to behold but completely unfamiliar.

I am not attempting the "slowing down" that starts with the TV remote and the couch. That one I know. I want the slowing down that empties and airs out, that silences inner chatter. The nondistracting, settling kind of nothing. The kind that makes you remember things you thought you'd long forgotten. The kind that brings acuity.

It is what I crave—stillness, long enough to hear the sound of my own heartbeat once again, to reconfirm or at least understand what it is beating for. The answers lie before me like a crossword puzzle or quantum physics, cooing and cautioning. Pandora's box.

I toy with "nothing" here under the winter sun, working it over and over, wondering, considering, trying to wring a drop of the mystery out of my parched soul. It gives me something to do while I relax.

Chapter Three

Sitting Still

I made a promise to myself before I got here: *Stop each day, no matter what I am doing, and observe every sunrise and every sunset.* The sunsets—not a problem. Now the sunrises . . . well, for a sleepless night owl—major commitment. The past few mornings, I've felt like I have sandpaper on the inside of my eyelids. If it weren't for Starbucks' Italian Roast, I'd utterly fail.

It's so still at dawn. Even the scavenger seagulls refuse to budge.

This morning, I fight to keep my eyes open as I reach for the doorknob. The sounds of the Gulf erupt in windy swells, vacillating in pitch and filter. I strain to hear their nuances, and for a moment it sounds like layer upon layer of a string symphony. Ethereal chords undulating, ebbing and flowing in delightful tension. It is the music I have heard in my dreams late at night only every once in a great while. Symphonies in the surf. I never knew where that music came from. Lush soundscapes in the early morning silence— a treasure, a perk to the attuned heart. So peaceful. So centering. And to think it has been like this here every day—365 days a year— for centuries now.

I feel my spirit give an inward sigh of connection. This is now home base. This is my soul airing out. Just as fully as I feel connected to this moment, I recognize a tiny obvious principle I've never noticed before: how simple it truly is, the connection of God's creation with God's creation. My spirit to His sea. My eyes to His sun. My toes to His sand. My mind to His intricate designs in the hermit crabs, in the palm leaves, in the veined stone. It was all meant to be. My eyes were made to behold, to appreciate, His creation. It brings me a sense of completion, inner rest, when I do it. My mind was made to toy with, to grasp and enjoy, His creation. It calms me when I rest my mind on His intricate designs and "art."

How odd that all these years, instead of looking out the window or breathing in His fragrance in flowers and wet earth, I have reached for a slim plastic box that turns on another bigger plastic box that projects man-dictated images into my house. Plastic, fabrication, an assault on the senses—the ears, the eyes, the soul— because it is all so imperfect and devoid of what true beauty, true detox, looks like: God's creation beholding God's creation.

It's why the surf sounds so wonderful to me right now. It's why the salt in the air feels good against my skin. It's why what I was doing in the past to satisfy and air out has not worked. The lifestyle I was trying to embrace wasn't designed for the way I was designed. It was second best, a counterfeit.

God's peace is all around me now. It is almost shouting at me, yet I go into my house and watch a plastic box in order to regroup and wind down. It's a big, simple concept discovered so early on in my stay. Perhaps God is chatty after all.

* * *

I head back out to the splintered wooden deck for another attempt at "detox." I manage to sit for two hours, staring at the water, but I feel like someone whose senses have been plugged into a wall outlet. Too much coffee. Six cups. I want to wag my head from side to side and giggle maniacally as I sit. *It's the caffeine*, I tell myself, *nothing worse*. But I am quite afraid that maybe I have lost the ability to completely shut off. I have these tiny reprieves where I'm able to crawl out of my skin and feel the world for a moment without any of my baggage in tow, but as quickly as they happen, they disappear. I seem to have no control over their emergence or exit. *But I am sticking to it*, I tell myself. *This will work itself out and I will relax*, I inwardly chant as I grip the arms of the gray chair tighter.

I force myself to stay outside, disciplined and determined, for hours, until midway through hour three I see them: porpoises. Three in a line, arcing toward the sky in synchronicity. I've never seen them "in person" before, only on TV.

I've always seen things "audibly." To me, everything in life has a soundtrack. Every life has a theme song. The porpoises are a slightly spirited version of Pachelbel's "Canon in D," the piece that people play at weddings as everyone is seated. I've always thought it fitting when the selection is used that way because it sends a subliminal message: "Slow down. Understand the meaning of the day. Be present in it. This will take time. Mark each step. Feel your purpose in the procession. Enjoy the moment."

It's the same message I am hearing now as the porpoises glint in the early morning sun. Their slow, rhythmic dance slightly calms me. Sparkling like diamonds in the distance, their black skin flashes light. I am uncovered by it. It reveals me harried. I've been living too fast, but then I don't even know if you can call it "life" at that speed.

Chapter Four

Digging Down

S ome things are worth digging for, even if they come up swing-
ing when they are unearthed.

This afternoon, I take my shoes off and dig my feet into the
sand down by the waterline. The sand is so much colder than my
skin that it feels wet. The shock of it feels good. Hugging my knees
to my chest, I study the wake.

When I was small, we went to Fire Island every weekend. I sat
just like this, studying the tiny air bubbles that pop up in the sand
as the water recedes. According to my brother, they were airholes for
hermit crabs burying themselves in the sand. I remember digging
up a few crabs and getting pinched for the effort. They look the
same to me now, appearing and vanishing as the waves wash them
smooth.

I don't know what day it is today. I took off my watch days ago.
My wrist feels unnaturally light.

I've heard about people getting lost like this. They sit and watch
these very same things until they become whole again.

I wonder what they see.

• • •

It's amazing what has already become secondary since I first arrived here, like combing my hair (scary but true). I haven't watched the news. I haven't looked at a calendar. I haven't tried to match my socks to my shoes—or even to each other on some days. I haven't eaten much either. What an interesting fact it is that when I am alone, I'm not particularly hungry. All these years I've been trying to diet, and maybe I just needed some space! But when I do have a craving, like right now, it's always for something salty and bad, like what they feed you on airplanes.

The last time I flew, I started one of those annoying math questions that appear on aptitude tests: "If train A leaves the Columbus station en route to New York at a speed of fifty miles an hour and train B leaves the same station 20 minutes later . . ." Only mine was about how many flight segments I ride in a year and how many small bags of peanuts and pretzels I consume proportionately. I believe I calculated somewhere between 125-150 bags per year—if the flight attendants don't offer leftovers, in which case, my total might be slightly more.

And that explains why I am never hungry when I finally get where I am going. I am so bloated from junk that I don't have another inch to spare. I know I should eat proper food, but I am too stuffed. There's no room for it. I find myself living for digestion, which never seems to come because when I should be just about empty, I am on a return flight home and the bags are dispensed again.

I'm bundled up in a sweater, with two pairs of baggy socks on, staring at the flickering light in the fireplace. The doors facing the Gulf are wide open. The sound of the waves is the backdrop for the crackling wood. The heat is off, and I'm digesting.

I realize that although I have been full for many years, I've been starving. I've been bloated from the familiar segment of life that keeps being served up. I've been out of balance, and my soul has been malnourished as a result. The full scope of what I should be experiencing has been shoved aside in the name of efficiency. Future and all it takes to prepare its place have taken over the present. I've been so forward-looking that I've missed the everyday things, I think.

I shift positions on the couch as I consider what I am beginning to see. It's just a shadow now, a phantom, but somehow I think it's what I am here to face. I feel as if my own skin is miles away. My life puffs out to its edges, but my soul is like a tiny pea shriveled in its center.

How did I get here?

* * *

I spend the morning watching *Columbo* while playing Solitaire just so I can feel productive. I cheated myself, and although I won, it was hollow. It's not very Columbo-like to cheat.

There are two ladies who look to be in their seventies walking down the beach, two medium-sized square blocks of life leaning into the icy breeze. The wind licks their clothes across the front of their bodies as they move east. They are lost in their individual thoughts, not even talking. In fact, they aren't even looking at one another.

The wind is wafting off the Gulf right through my French doors, and with it comes the first sound the women on the beach make. It is a call: "Viiiiiiiinnnnnnnnnnnnneeeeeeeeeey!" One woman bends at the waist and claps her hands. The call continues, "Vinny! Vinny!" followed by warmer tones and indistinguishable cooing.

All at once, I see Vinny. He is a huge, well-groomed, full-sized white poodle. He looks as if he is in circus wear with his pom-poms and puffy ears. A yellow tennis ball sails into the frigid Gulf water, and Vinny springs forward, trained on it as if it were a mallard. He is moving like a hunter, head remaining high above the waves. They crash down on his muzzle with a slap, washing over his manicured ears more than a few times. He continues forward. He likes the challenge. The women encourage him with their shrill cheers.

Somewhere in the back of my mind, I remember a special about poodles on the Discovery Channel—how they are hunters, how their elaborate hairdos are actually designed to protect the vital organs of the body should they retrieve in cold water. Seemed a little far-fetched when I considered my childhood friend's miniature poodle, Jackie. That dog was a housekeeper's nightmare. If you just looked at her, she would pee on the carpet. Even in a purely affectionate sense, she was subpar. There was hardly anything to pet.

Not so with Vinny. He prances up the shore, tennis ball gleaming in his dainty mouth. He drops it obediently, shakes his fur. Water goes everywhere, spraying on the women. This causes eruptive laughter and still another toss that makes me jealous. I wonder if I've ever thrown that far in my life.

We all come here to the shore, young and old, poodles and golden retrievers, dolphins and herons, Yankees and Southerners. We come prissy, duplicitous, all tucked in and worn out. We come with our heaviness, and our questions, and our disappointments, and our loves. We breathe more deeply, stare more fervently, feel less carefully. We laugh more easily and see more clearly—and play if we're lucky.

Unlike the common anesthesia we seek in our normal lives—the things that remove us from our own skin—we find a new kind, one that blots out the unimportant concerns, one that draws us closer to life's stimulus. An anesthesia that does not edit but rather empowers. One that reminds us of how fresh the breeze can be, how awesome a storm can seem, how little and endless our lives truly are, and especially how the small things are the true things sometimes. God's entertainment. God's provision for our ragged souls. The distant echo of all that is meaningful and eternal, apparently to dogs *and* people alike.

* * *

"Aha!" I puff out on the next morning's walk, the way Sherlock Holmes used to when he discovered a clue. I startle myself with the forcefulness in my own voice at this early hour. With each passing day, I think these early morning hikes are getting a little easier—at least that's what I keep telling myself.

I am already thinking clearly today. The bitter cold has iced my ears over, but I won't cover them. It would defeat the purpose that I came here for: to hear the surf. Yesterday was like finally finding a match in a dark cave. I found enough light to know I was in the cave and wasn't in immediate danger.

This morning, as I sit silently before the sun, an old cartoon flashes into my mind. It was all about a carrot. I've never forgotten the cartoon image of a donkey, back bowed from overuse, blinders on his eyes, straw hat, walking eternally toward a carrot that is hung at the end of a makeshift fishing pole, forever dangling just out of his reach. It's close enough to smell and, on uphill treks, almost close enough to bite—but never truly his.

The donkey is so consumed with making contact with the carrot that he does not object to the cart attached to his harness or the weight of those in the cart who hold the carrot. He strains, but he doesn't care. He's just going where he's led by the carrot. And if he ever *does* get the carrot, it will be long after the drivers have used him up getting what they want—his strength, his determination, his efforts—for their gain.

That's the trick (all cartoons have one). The donkey doesn't know he is being used. He doesn't know that less than two feet away is all the grass he could ever want or that he is passing by trees with fruit far sweeter. His eyes remain trained on the carrot, and they are focused that way because someone wanted them that way. Someone defined his sight line. Someone gave him a template to see through. He has one definition of happiness, one definition of success—and *someone else* gave him that definition.

I always felt sorry for the donkey character. If he only knew what he was passing up for something he would never possess.

I wonder what I've let other people define for me.

. . .

Something deep and incisive punctured me this morning, and my world tilted. It all started yesterday with the hurricane. A hurricane is beautiful when it first starts. Like a heavy, dark, sodden curtain, the sky drops down. Streaks of light peek through the cracks as the rain comes horizontally, propelled by the wind. And here through these windows, I am able to see how big bodies of water respond. The surf kicks up into a frenzy, whitecaps throwing themselves in the air in fragmented explosions.

The chaos was fun at first, but then it hit me that I hadn't seen any other human being in a while. As the mayhem progressed, I went out to the street. There was not a light on as far as I could see. That's when I understood that this beautiful rainstorm was probably something more sinister.

I went in and turned on the Weather Channel. My area came up, and there were evacuation warnings. A hurricane was approaching fast. I had that moment of wondering what to do, which is always a horrible time to make a critical decision. I hate moments like that—when you have ten seconds to make a decision that will impact your life profoundly. I had no idea what the proper evacuation route would be. I had no idea who to call or even if it were too late to call.

In a split second, I put all the particulars aside. Maybe it was the fact that I was rested—or maybe just foolhardy. I always said I wanted to die in my sleep, so I just went to bed.

And I slept.

I woke early, even without an alarm clock. There was water throughout the house, blown in under the doors by the wind. The beach was disheveled and tossed with boards, branches, and things long lost at sea like old buoys. The patio furniture was all over the beach, and my sunglasses were nowhere to be found.

Before dawn I sat on the couch facing east, with my usual cup in hand, ready for the sunrise. There was no power, so I had to settle for water instead of coffee. Still, I was wide awake.

Before the sun became visible, the most magnificent hues of orange and red floated upward in thin horizontal stripes. Rising like heralds, each line was more fiery and artistic than the last. The sky behind them slowly transformed from black to deep shades of blue. When the sun finally arrived, it was an orange shimmering ball, steadily rising, majestic and unstoppable, like a King in all His glory.

The whole ascension was so radiant that I found myself fighting back tears. Perfectly random. Recklessly precise. So beyond me. So far above me. By the end of the sunrise, I was on my feet cheering, laughing, and crying—all at the same time. My response was spontaneous, instinctual almost. I was so full in that moment, so overwhelmed, that I felt as though my soul would burst out of my chest and fly away. I was *there*, I realized. Fully there. It was another gem of a realization during my visit so far. The fullness brought to mind a favorite psalm:

In thy presence is fullness of joy; at thy right hand there are pleasures for evermore.[1]

Fullness of joy. Not just joy, but *fullness* of joy. Full: To be not only satiated but also satisfied. There in the beach chaos came a demonstration of God's power—His immutable elegance, so irrefutable, in the midst of what seemed to be destruction. God Himself rose before my eyes, hinting the beautiful principle of new beginnings through purging, through hardship, through seeming destruction. That premise, coming to life before my eyes in the sunrise, gave me "fullness of joy." And as I considered the rest of the Scripture, I recognized for the first time the very simple premise I've understood but not "known."

In thy presence. That is the only place we can experience the fullness of joy: in God's presence. I was in His presence this morning. Right there, in a moment where nothing could interfere, not the telephone, not even the coffeemaker. Nothing but an allegorical picture of His redemption, granted by a terrible storm and an empty "space." I was there—present. He was there. I experienced His presence. And I had fullness of joy—enough to get me to my feet cheering His display—and I'm not even Pentecostal!

And to think that *that* type of display happens every day, all the time.

Where have I been?

• • •

The hurricane has left a gray pallor over the beach. Even the seagulls are staying away. But I like the rain, for a time anyway. This morning the sun is a dull gray smudge, willing itself up. It is Bach's "Agnus Dei" from his *Mass in B Minor*, beautiful and mournful, punished by the elements, but triumphant at last over all.

Thinking of "Agnus Dei" takes me immediately back to the many years of voice lessons I took at Mr. Falk's house. It was there, at fourteen, that I first had the pleasure of meeting that work and the elite task of learning it.

Mr. Falk was just about what you'd expect. Old—at least I

think. Of course, everyone seems old to a high school freshman. Now that I think about it, he was probably in his midfifties. Not *that* old really. Let's just say mature. He had the kind of appearance you see in theatre makeup: full sand-colored beard streaked with gray, thick unruly eyebrows, black horn-rimmed glasses. And he smelled of sweet pipe tobacco. I always envisioned him in caricature, hunched over his piano, with a sharp, dusty varnish scent rising from the yellowed ivory keys. I'd imagine curls of steam coming out of his ears as he "emoted" in the language he loved best, the muted sonorous strokes of felt on steel.

In my make-believe world, this type of concentration emits radiation of some kind, which would explain the two bald patches that streaked down the right and left side of his skull. It was the "tortured artist" look—long shock of hair in the center, the resulting pattern formed by the heat of too many intense thoughts and rapturous arpeggios.

Mr. Falk was elegant, as was his house, where on Tuesday nights at seven I would stand next to his baby grand and make animal sounds. "Ying, ying, ying" and "mmmmmmmmwaaaaaaaaahhhhhh." The latter left me looking like I had a bad case of lockjaw.

He led the charge with a deep resonant voice that could bring you to tears or make your fillings rattle. Up and down the scale we went together in all sorts of musical contortions. Sometimes his dog, Puccini, would howl along with me. I never knew if this was an uncontrollable effort to participate in my beautiful interpretations or just sheer pain. I was lopping the head off of high C in those days. I do believe that range is dog territory.

With my classical music book folded over the shift lever of the handlebars, I rode my three-speed Schwinn knockoff to Mr. Falk's house, pedaling furiously through the elements. Rain, sleet, snow, dark—it didn't matter, I was there. I couldn't get there fast enough or early enough because, as far as I understood it, that music book held my future. Over the years, the zealousness of my grip on the book as I rode wore a hole right through the back cover and into Mozart's "Non So Più."

I knew as an adolescent what success was to me: to make music. And no one told me. That template came from inside of me. I felt it in the deepest places that one can feel, and I felt good every time I thought about it. I was in some sort of natural life flow, a frictionless environment where everything aligns and you have deep sight. I knew what I wanted, and I knew what I had to do to get it. I wanted to sing, and I had to learn those songs in order to learn how to sing. I would have quacked like a duck for six days straight if I thought it would have given me stronger vocal chords.

The remembrance calms me now in the hurricane, like a tiny light projecting coded messages: "Come back. I'm still here. You remember how to get here."

A new strike of thunder illuminates the violent waves momentarily. I wish again for that time, that journey, that clarity. It was a peaceful time in my life.

I don't know what it all means. I only know that on some level, I'm remembering things long forgotten, things that I believe will show me again who I am and what I need.

* * *

I jogged to the Hilton later this morning for some breakfast and saw a group of "snowbirds" in the outdoor pool. Forty degrees out. They must be from Michigan.

In their bathing suits and rubber caps, all shapes and sizes, they were having a blast, looking more like kids than like retirees. I want to be like that.

Watching them from the patio, I drained the last of my coffee, thinking about how self-conscious I feel in my bathing suit. The thought came in the form of "inner chatter," the kind that comes in your own voice. Mine was saying something like, *If I were ten pounds thinner, I'd be tempted to put my suit on and join them. But not today. Someday soon.*

I stopped mid-sentence. A light went on inside of me, revealing a dimension I'd never noticed before. I'd never noticed it because it's always been with me, a part of me, like a heart or a kidney. It's grown as I've grown.

Inner chatter. Negative inner chatter. A spoiler's voice. Sentences that begin with, *"When I _____ "* and end with *"then I will _____ ."* And *"If I _____ , then _____ will happen."*

I mentally turned around in my brain only to see an invisible line stemming from that thought to a million others like it. What I *couldn't* do. Why I *shouldn't* do it. What *wasn't* up to par. What *wouldn't* ever be good enough or strong enough. So many random thoughts, and very few were life-giving or accurate. All of them caused me to live "edited." Not to try. Not to enjoy. Not to move with confidence.

I cringed as I realized the truth of it. *When did I start stuffing myself into a tiny definition of beauty? Why can't I wear that bathing suit? What is the matter with me? Whose standard of beauty have I been embracing? Whose standard of confidence am I assuming? Whose life rules am I following as I decide whether or not to live passionately, free from conformity?*

The swirling thoughts nauseated me, like watching a super-speed playback on video, until I came to a dead stop at a more cruel truth: the opportunity missed, fun not had, living left unlived, clothes unworn, swims not taken, glances shied away from, and time—precious, unsalvageable time—wasted from my living in the phantom shadow of "when" and "if."

This had been my life of late: the real forfeited for the imagined, the actual for the anticipated. I was sure that on some level this was all an insult to God. He gave me the "present moment." I eschewed it in favor of something else, somewhere else. He gave me my body, anomalies and all, and I had somehow come to the conclusion that it wasn't good enough.

Sin is a word that usually conjures up visions of murder, lust, impropriety. It hardly ever brings the picture of its actual definition, simply translated from the Greek word *hamartia* as "missing the mark." It can be as uneventful as aiming for one thing when you should be aiming for another, or doing things partially that should be done fully. In light of that, I am sure this halfhearted, quietly fearful living is sin.

Scriptures I have long loved come suddenly to life:

The LORD will fulfill his purpose for me;
your love, O LORD, endures forever—
do not abandon the works of your hands.[2]

I am fearfully and wonderfully made.[3]

He had no beauty or majesty to attract us to him.[4]

God created us all in His image. He created us individually to be a part of both a central and an individual purpose. When we feel uncomfortable in our own skin, it's as if we are saying that God made a mistake. We are not right somehow. The end result is that we are then judging God—His handiwork—and then we are God and He is not.

Have I gotten so out of whack that I have been judging God, silently, unknowingly—and refusing His presence, His provision—as a result of being so distracted? I saw the cartoon donkey again in my mind's eye. Tingling and stunned, I put a twenty under the saltshaker and slowly descended the stairs to the beach. I staggered toward my house drunk with sight. So rare, these moments of revelation—rare and uncontrived.

On my way home, my arms hung more loosely at my sides. I knew something now—a beginning at least. I don't know how I knew, other than by divine lightning bolts piercing my brain. I considered the knowledge, examined it and its gravity. I spread my arms wide to the truth, and right there in public I fell to my knees, tipped my head back, and prayed out loud:

Forgive me, God. Forgive my idols. Forgive my stupidity.
Show me what is real. Teach me what is beautiful. Rend the
veil on my soul. Help me live to the outer limits of my senses,
unedited, free in your grace.

Chapter Five

Ready to Exhale

I couldn't fully shut off the shower this morning. The head drib-bled water for about an hour and then made the transition to fat, sporadic drips. It reminded me of the leak in my laundry room. It was the intermittent kind, easy to ignore.

Leaks are evil. I despise them. They are subtle and elusive. Behind the facade, they slowly erode away structure and integrity in secret—unhampered, unchecked. By the time the evidence of their hideous mission announces itself outwardly, the majority of the damage is done.

I learned this the day the damp spot on my ceiling at home swelled from a quarter to a pancake. I got up on the step stool to inspect. Tentatively raising my pointer finger to feel the level of dampness, I touched the pancake ever so gently. The brown patch gave way, and all at once my entire hand was swallowed up into the netherworld of pipes and insulation. Just one tiny push, and drywall rudely crumbled onto my face, sending me sputtering and swaying.

It's odd what you think about in moments like that. I had two distinct things on my mind as I clung to balance: *"If I fall and break my neck, how long will it be before someone comes to find me?"* and *"Betrayer!"*

I was miffed with the drywall. I saw it as a conspirator. All these years, I'd contentedly trusted it with its responsibility to hide all those things I didn't need to know about and to retain the magic of all those things I took for granted. Underneath our beautiful lives together, I washed enough towels and jeans to drain Lake Meade. It's seen me first thing in the morning without makeup, even naked. We had a relationship!

I trusted that drywall. I counted on it. I was convinced that if it knew something bad might be afoot, it would have immediately let me know. Not with some tiny indication, like the little dot of off-white stain that appeared about six months ago—no. Surely it could've served up the pancake a little more quickly, maybe thrown in an alarming color like rust or black.

When I removed my hand, I saw everything I didn't care to know about, and the knowing made me responsible for it. That is how I feel about what's been happening since I "escaped" my former life: I poked a hole in the façade, and now the drywall is crumbling down.

There seems no end to it. With each thought comes another, and then another—a million things connected to a million other things. Things like permission. My "whens" and "ifs" are based upon permission. Waiting for permission to do something. Waiting for someone or something to give me permission—to live, to try, to be. I am a full-grown adult, yet somewhere in my pipes I've been waiting for permission to flow.

At what age do you stop needing permission? And this permission—is it a leftover from the childhood mission to "lay low and be obedient"? Did I learn it so well then that it is running through my entire infrastructure now, unable to retire itself? Am I so busy doing what's "right" and expected that I am missing the personal journey divinely laid out for me? Am I missing the one I will learn from, enjoy, and be transformed by? Am I doing what I should be doing—for me? Am I in *my* rightful place?

I wonder if it's been easier to wrap myself up in expectations—other people's expectations of what my life should stand for, what it should look like—than it would have been to determine these things for myself. There is a certain degree of safety in relying on other people to do the determining for you. If you can't fulfill it, it is much easier to blame it on the "system" or the "expectation" than it is to admit that it was you, and you alone, who set the standard for yourself—and, perhaps, who failed it. It's easier, I think, to be safe than it is to understand your own personal life's infrastructure. It's easier to not know than it is to labor to learn.

That's why I believe we like ceremony and absolutes in areas that may need to be more spontaneous and interactive. It takes courage to have an ongoing, interactive dialogue about these things with Christ. It takes courage to make a determination and move forward or backward based on it. It takes courage to fail and adjust. Am I that brave?

Am I, am I, am I?

I've got to turn it around and begin here:

I am . . .
I am undone.
It's a start.

• • •

I woke peacefully today. There's something about being undone that ends up being ultimately relaxing, like the feel of a sneaker when it's untied or last night's blouse strewn over a chair—they have function, but for now, they're just resting.

From where I sit, I can see herons busy at work securing breakfast.

Gliding stealthily over the Gulf, inches from the surface, they hunt. The sight of their wings fanning up and down in slow motion reminds me of the way I fly in my dreams—effortlessly. They sound like Adiemus's "Adiemus": Regal, focused. Gracefully strong.

They have their mission: to eat. Every fiber of their being is fully present in that mission, in that moment. They are living the present. They have no thought of yesterday, no worries about tomorrow.

In thy presence is fullness of joy.

One heron suddenly drops perpendicular and pierces the water with hardly a splash. Seconds later, he exits with a large fish in his gullet.

"Consider the ravens: They do not sow or reap, they have no storeroom or barn; yet God feeds them. And how much more valuable you are than birds!"[5]

The eight-year-old in me wonders if the heron feels content or relieved or accomplished. I wonder if that kind of dependence on the natural "playing out" of life under God's watchful eye is innate in wild birds. Is His presence so ingrained in their lives that they can trust it like we trust a chair to hold our weight—no question, no consideration, just second nature?

The adult in me has no idea how the hunting bird feels. I haven't had that kind of focus on the present moment in a long time. I decide I want to start making it a habit.

I have read that repentance is a sudden cessation of one direction and the pursuit of another. To stop, adjust, and go another way. To cease and become, all in one action. I guess you could say the heron repented of flying and went after his fish.

I will repent of rushing and go after mine.

• • •

The sea has still not reclaimed what the storm dredged up. Old beach chairs, fishing nets, and a fresh crop of weathered shells and wood still litter the sand drifts.

I collected driftwood on my walk this morning, branches and boards weathered smooth. I gathered so many that I had to stop three times on the route back, winded from the weight of them. There's something about their starkness that I can't resist.

I laid them out on the deck for now, but once I return home—unless Martha Stewart tells me what to do with them—I suspect they will go the way of *Forbes Magazine.* They'll sit in a pile and wait to be the focus of my free time for about three years. I'll move them around my house until I'm embarrassed about them, and eventually I'll throw them out.

Every morning for days now, I've been mentally picking at the mass that is my life, trying to find the one loose thread that will untangle the ball. What I am looking for, I don't even know. I walk the shore and ask myself indulgent questions like, *Am I happy? Have I accomplished what I set out to do? Am I the person I want to be? Am I doing what I was designed to do? Will I regret not being more adventurous with my life? Or have I become too safe? Am I hemming myself in? Am I making the best use of my life? Does what I am doing count for anything?*

I walk and pick, wondering if these questions are truly what pulled me here. *Do I have a right to ask them?*

And in my wondering, I go back to my basics: the things I learned as a child, simple techniques to solve most of life's problems. I remember the surefire way my older sister, Kate, used to get to the bottom of anything. She'd get a piece of paper and draw a vertical line down its center, creating two equal halves. On one side she would write the heading "Pros" and on the other "Cons." As though she were Walter Cronkite, she'd interview me to the tiniest detail, writing every answer down, making sure not to repeat a concept.

I wish she were here now. I can envision her with pen and yellow legal pad in hand, "What has gone good in my life" on one side of the long sheet and "What is bugging me (not so good)" on the other. Then on the next page, "Dreams that have come true" and "Things I still would like to try."

In the end, the "formula" would yield a simple number that gave the answer to the overall health of my situation. If there were more pros than cons, then I was all right. If I had more "good" things in my life than "annoyances," I was on the right track.

I employ Kate's technique, right down to the headings and the bisecting line. But the problem is, I don't know what to write in my columns. I don't even know what questions to ask. I'm not even sure if I have the right to ask them. Somehow, they seem on the edge of selfish, yet I know they can't be entirely so.

There's that permission thing again. I decide that I do have a right to ask.

Breathing Deep

*God gave us the gift of life; it is up to us
to give ourselves the gift of living well.*

—VOLTAIRE

Chapter Six

Dreaming Wide

Lost my mind today at the "Super K."
I sort of went into a buying frenzy. On my way to the sunblock, I got a whiff of fresh paper, crayons, pencils—all the things that reek of ideas not realized, possibilities not explored, thoughts not voiced. Stopping dead in my tracks at the top of the office aisle, I had the familiar sinking feeling I had in any five-and-dime store as a kid—the one about not being able to buy what I want, because everything always cost about twenty-five cents more than I had.

Then, all at once, it hit me: *I am an adult. I have an American Express! I can buy anything and everything I want. Nothing is out of my reach!* So I went at it: a big sketchpad, colored markers, scissors, a ruler, some magazines, a stick of glue, oil pencils, crayons, and a miniature television-set pencil sharpener whose screen was an optical illusion that changes when you move the object slightly. In this case, I had a cat that winked at me.

I bought candy too. Necco wafers, Almond Joy, Bazooka bubblegum, Sweet Tarts—just enough to feel decadent.

It would've been easier to shop with a basket, but I ignored the urge, afraid it would rouse the adult in me. I didn't want to come back to my senses and make myself put my loot back. I just kept grabbing stuff and loading it up until it was overflowing out of my arms.

I piled it all onto the counter, and the salesperson gave me that, "Oh, what a great mom to be buying all of this for her child" look. With a wink she queried, "Big project at home, huh?" Still in my sweats, recklessly pillow-bald on the left side of my head, I dead-panned back, "The biggest."

I wasn't sure what that project would be. All I knew was I wanted to get back into that place of dreaming, the same zone that coloring used to take me—that place where all things seemed possible, time was endless, and a good day's work consisted of bringing another page to life with color.

Coloring has always been a total "check-out" activity for me. I haven't done it for years now, but this reckless usage of time, this non-adult fun, got me completely out of my adult self for a while. Something about concentrating on spreading waxy tones on paper is freeing. Getting the green exactly where the stalk of the sea grass meets the plume. Making the shade of worn wood from browns and grays, and for the first time seeing the white that is in it—a noncolor—highlighting the peaks of a monochromatic jumble.

I tried to take my coloring to a new height this morning, one I suspect crayons were never meant to achieve. Still, the attempt has caused me to scrutinize common things that I take for granted, common tones in life. I am finding details in objects that never appeared so intricate before, and the "seeing" has set off an odd dimension shift for me.

I wonder if that is what Jesus was talking about when He said, "I tell you the truth, unless you change and become like little children, you will never enter the kingdom of heaven."[6] The scary, simple attitude of trust that approaches life's troubles and riddles with peaceful assurance, trust that makes no orderly sense, trust that is based on one premise alone: that God said it, so it is.

In the margins of these drawings, I begin writing random

thoughts, concerns, questions, dreams. I even write a small story about nothing. It starts the process that I have long needed—the examination of all the familiar things in my life, the process of trying to find the nuances and patterns I need to notice. In those patterns, I hope to rediscover the part of me that can trust like a child, the part that chooses absolute belief in spite of life experience or supposed knowledge, the part that stops off first at the promise of an eternal, loving Creator and *then* moves on to lesser things, like facts and obstacles.

In all of this, I know one thing for sure: It is based on the process of forgetting what I have taken for granted—both good and bad—and learning it fresh.

· · ·

What if my life were a fresh page? What if I could write it from this day forward, no holds barred? What if I could make plans and schemes that would actually affect things, knowing that God could interrupt my plans at any given moment if I were off track, or if He had something different in mind? That's what I considered as I tried to beat my all-time best stone's throw into the surf this afternoon.

I found the stones up in the dunes, brought them back to the surf line, and made a small pile. Waiting until the coast was clear of any walkers, I began my game. Seagulls took note and quickly gathered around me, hovering like a low-lying cloud. I think they thought I was throwing out last night's dinner.

The first few throws landed my left sneaker in the surf. I never noticed that I do a little hop and skip to the side before I release my grip. If I were playing basketball, I think it would be called traveling. I'm sure it's some leftover lucky charm propulsion technique I acquired during the many baseball games I played in the street on Long Island.

I'd thrown almost all of the stones when I heard a little click in my shoulder, followed by a dull pain. I know it well. Feels like my shoulder is coming off its hinge. I begrudgingly stopped, sitting down in the sand to rest.

I hate getting old.

I'm going to fill up blank paper this afternoon, writing stories—not just any stories, but my story, played out in a number of different ways.

My only rule is to approach it like a biographer, as if someone is documenting my life from death backward. I'll recall all the details that would be included in such an accounting, except that it will be the *Reader's Digest* version.

First, I'll write it like I have no knowledge of what I can't do, writing like I believe I am capable of all things. If Kate were here, she'd title it "My Wildest Dreams." Then, if it doesn't stress me out, I'll write the way it actually has been, taking into account my fears and perceived limitations. I'll carry out my present life to its logical conclusion, just as it has been lived up until now. "If I change nothing, this is probably what I will be doing twenty years from now . . ." Kate would title that something like "Reality."

I won't edit. I am going to just write. I don't know if I'll capitalize or punctuate or even indent. I think I'll just be messy about it, do it in crayon, with my "wrong hand," so I will truly have to concentrate on what I mean.

I'm going to write it out in time increments, like "One year from now, I will be . . ." I will finish out the story however it occurs to me, but I'll cover details like where I'll be living, what I'll be doing, what I will look like, how I will feel, what my accomplishments will be, who my friends will be, what I will be doing to relax, and other things that might seem important to note. Then I will write that same story for five, ten, twenty, thirty, forty—even fifty years from now.

And if the whole exercise starts to feel even remotely like work, I'm going to go into the house to watch *Columbo* and eat Sweet Tarts.

Chapter Seven

My Life Stories— Part 1

T he shells I gleaned from the beach this morning are laid out in a perfect horizontal line at my feet. Hermit crab shells perfectly made. Beautiful.

I rub my eyes as the winter sun arcs higher overhead. I am having lofty thoughts on this Saturday afternoon—I don't know where they're going to take me. I feel dangerous even considering such anarchist concepts as the ones that have filled my paper. I didn't even know some of these things were on my radar. I don't know whether to laugh or to call a psychiatrist when I read them over.

My Life Stories
Wildest Dreams Version
Ten Years from Now

- I will have a golden retriever because I'm home long enough to housebreak him.
- I will have enough money to travel on short jaunts when I want to and will have a dear friend who can babysit my golden retriever.

- I will be more concentric, surrounding myself with people I love.

In the wide margins of my page I've scribbled notes to myself here and there, as quickly and freely as they've come to mind.

Who do I know now that I will want in my life then? What a strange thing that I've never considered this before. I guess it was yet another thing that just blurred into the scheme of things— people are just "there," relationships just "are," by blood, proximity, sometimes choice. I wonder why I've never thought about securing them, consciously thought about investing in them.

I suppose it's another side issue that stems from being single. Of course people invest in their marriages, their kids, but even married people have relationships outside of their marriage—good ones. On some level, we are all dependent on community to survive. Everyone faces loss, and whether it leaves you an orphan or a widow, the blow leaves a hole. Community comes in there. Why haven't I invested more heavily in the community God has blessed me with?

- I will continue some relationships for sure and secure them at all costs, but I know that some will naturally morph into something and somewhere else. And that will be okay.
- I will eat out more for celebratory reasons, and I will learn how to cook for entertaining purposes—*really* cook, so people don't have to be polite at my table.
- I will have 24 percent body fat and most of my own teeth. I will wear polyester pants only if they are in style, not because I *have* to.

I never saw this as an investment either, but what a big fat concept! Literally! If I don't take the time to do what is right for my body, then how will I ever be confident, energized, ready for what I

*am supposed to be in this world in the future? And this has to begin
now—here—in order to secure the strength and vitality that will
allow me to be healthy, to move and walk from my own power.
No fries tonight. Tough.*

- Working out will be a priority to me because I want to live
  confidently and, for me, having a strong, healthy body has a
  lot to do with that.
- I'm not sure if I will be living in my current house, although
  it wouldn't bother me if I were.
- I will be traveling lightly for business because I will have
  shifted my income base to mostly writing sources in order to
  work from home in my pajamas if I so desire.
- I won't hold back when I laugh, anytime—especially in
  public—because I'll be almost old or at least pushing mature
  and won't want to waste time being careful.
- I think I will throw my head back when I do laugh, and open
  my mouth very wide so that the roof of my mouth shows.
- When someone is sad, I will stop everything I'm doing and
  be sad with them. I'll hold hands a little longer than is tradi-
  tionally comfortable. And I will hug like old aunts do, too
  long and too strong. But I will have fresh breath.
- I will be earthy and a bit eccentric, but I will be wise.
- I will continue to resist buying anything from the Cracker
  Barrel gift shop.
- I will have a peace that emanates from understanding my
  place in life. And my faith will be the center of that peace. I
  will determine what is true for me within the context of my
  faith—from my own search, not just from the models that
  have been held up for me as true and ideal.
- I will be content in my individual "discovered" relationship
  with Christ.

- I will use my resources to feed children in need.
- I will have fed 500,000 of them.
- I will work at what pleases me, and I will find a way to make a living from it.

. . .

My pencil box came with a plastic magnifying glass. I've been using it for everything, from getting a better look at the shells I've gleaned to wearing it as a monocle when I run out of mind power. I'm working on my one-year paper, some of the elements I'd like to see come alive in the next twelve months. It's surprising to see how much of the next ten years will be set up by changes in the next year—if I can make them.

One Year from Now
- My house will be organized and the lawn will have actual grass on it.
- I will really learn how to cook—something, anything.
- I will begin to work on a book.
- I will be better at saying no, and I won't be doing work at all hours of the day and night. I will have gotten a hold of my schedule. All pertinent forces in my life will be adhering to my new schedule, which allows for some downtime—preferably, downtime without guilt.
- In work, I will say yes to the things that truly nourish me and others, and I will be better at saying no to things that take me off center. In fact, I will start working in a more focused and efficient manner on the things that count toward my long-term goals.
- I will save money and find someone to help me invest it productively.

- Mornings won't be rushed. I will spend a little extra time each morning gathering my thoughts and focusing.
- I will center my spiritual life by practicing the art of being present.

I need to figure out what is taking me out of the present moments in life. I am defaulting to things other than the moment, and I wonder if I can determine what they are and address them.

- I will not live harried. I *will* take downtime, and I will protect it.

This is something I should have in my DNA. My mom was great at this. When she had "enough," she would slowly walk to her bedroom, and just before the door closed, she would whisper, "Do not disturb me." Something about her high-language, delivered so dramatically, made it seem of the utmost importance, like something that nuns do. I remember my sister and I holding vigil quietly outside her door, rosary beads in hand, miming questions to each other and praying random prayers, scared to death that we sent her in there and she was deciding on appropriate punishment. Eventually, we'd resort to giggling, imitating how we'd fake-cry when she spanked us. Then she would hear us through the door. "I said!" is all she would declare, and that would be the last of it. We'd go back to whatever we had been doing before she'd sequestered herself, knowing that whatever it was that drove her in there was set in stone now.

We never did get disciplined when she came out. She just needed her space. She took it, for herself, and protected it. I need to find my ways of doing this.

- I will see my family more, and I will renew some relationships that have fallen by the wayside because of my schedule.
- I will begin to identify who is my support system and begin to pay closer attention to those relationships and invest in them.
- I will define and pursue my own definition of "success."
- I will be comfortable in my own skin—whatever that takes—and I will feed my soul.

* * *

Seems that everyone is talking about goals these days. It's big business, showing people how to meet them. In all my reading about goals, the one concept that's universal is "Don't overreach. Don't set yourself up for failure. Make goals you can reach with some ingénue and a little elbow grease."

Goals you can reach. By forward motion. It reminds me of a passage from *Alice's Adventures in Wonderland*: "It takes all the running *you* can do, to keep in the same place. If you want to get somewhere else, you must run at least twice as fast as that!"[7] I've never forgotten that—maybe because I always associated it with my best friend, Kevin, running up the wrong escalator at JC Penney as fast as he could, coming to a frenzied halt where he started, on the perpetual second step. That's how I've felt lately, like I just can't go any faster. I'm tired of running, and the last thing I need is another thing to do, at twice the speed.

Thinking about it exhausts me to the point of not wanting to go any further on any of this. Sail the Intercoastal in my golden years? Avoid polyester pants? I don't know if I can pull it off.

I guess my definition of *reachable* should be softened by the word *allowable*—allowable failure. "It's okay to fail." I'll just keep saying that to myself over and over in my therapist voice. It's not like I am hoping to become the president or an Olympic gymnast or something.

I need a nap.

. . .

Made some microwave popcorn this afternoon and set off the smoke alarm. I hope it's not connected to the fire station. I never can seem to get it right. It's that elusive five-second gap between the final few "pops" that always eludes me.

Hard, round kernels of soot—that's what most of it was when I was done. After sampling a handful, I walked the bag out to the edge of the dunes, where I turned it on its side and dropped popcorn pebbles from the burnt hole into the wind.

Immediately, I was surrounded by seagulls. In the mornings, they can't get away from me fast enough as I run by, but now, I am their friend. I wish people were that easy.

Some of the writing I've been doing has begun to remind me of everything I'm trying to leave behind for a time: stress, riddles, disappointments. It's hard to make the jump from the concerns to the solutions. I made the popcorn to break the spell.

My prayers have continued to stay simple since I've come here, and I have been wearing out a few in my top five. *Help me to be responsible to You. Help me to discern Your leading. Change me.*

I want to be sure that I am what I am supposed to be, that my life is continuing forward by the absolute guidance that God affords. I have a sense of urgency, a sense of gravity concerning the passing years and the imprint I will leave on this earth. I want to operate the way I was designed to operate, and flourish in God's calling on my life, whatever that is.

As the last bird tires of my empty bag, I make the first rule of my vacation: If it feels like work, looks like work, smells like work, or even slightly reminds me of work, I'm not doing it. I add an "Amen" to let God know it counts as a prayer, a rule made under His watchful eye, and is therefore revocable should He so desire.

The air is getting slightly chilly as the sun disappears. I turn my back to the sight and head back to the darkened house. I'm glad I stopped the stories. I don't want to rush this. I want to be as free as I can be. I'll dream more tomorrow, but only if I feel like it.

I'm starving now—forgot to eat lunch. The long wooden stairway to the house is a chore on my calves, which are still stiff from this morning's run. There are thirty-seven steps, a useless fact I determined the first day I walked them. Though I know the tally, the count begins again at step one. It's slow and steady, in a child's voice.

I haven't counted steps in decades. Maybe I am finally unwinding.

Chapter Eight

My Life Stories—
Part 2

I met George Anderson on the beach today. I've seen him walking a few times before. Older, toned. Eyes dead ahead, little one-pound weights pumping at his side. He means business.

We came together naturally as he exited the access path the same time I was walking by. We walked for a good hour. He dusted me.

Told him I was writing my thirty-year story today and asked for any wisdom he might have for me.

"Life flies by. Enjoy it."

"Thirty years from now" has always seemed like a fixed point in time when only other people lived. It's always felt like an experience that happens to only the people who are already right there, not those who observe from a safe distance. That false distance has made it easy to excuse myself from considering its occurrence in my own life. Excusing myself has led to an overall "wandering" technique as I inch toward it. I have barely given it a thought, other than the usual Social Security/retirement fund terror thoughts.

My Life Stories
Wildest Dreams Version
Thirty Years from Now

- I will be healthy.
- All the teeth that are visible will be my original set.

Gotta floss more.

- I will have enough money to live and maybe travel when I want to.

How much is enough? Hmmm. I believe I don't know how much is enough. Uh-oh. I'll worry about that later too.

- I will have a family around me.

Marriage? What if I am still single? Hmmm. I need to have an alternate plan in this area.

Who is in my life now that I want there in thirty years? Who will be sitting at my kitchen table at 10:00 a.m. for coffee? Who will I call at 2:00 p.m. for idle chatter? Who will come at midnight if I am alone and need to go to the hospital?

Who will have been around for my whole story and have years of perspective on me?

I know that Scripture speaks clearly and encouragingly about solitary people—the widows, the orphans—and how God sets them in families.[8] And the first response of the church to Christ's sacrifice was to form one big community,[9] to provide for one another, to share and function like a true body. I know it, but do I know it? Do I trust that it is real and not just a "consolation prize" but rather God's actual provision—His path for me?

Definitely need people, love people.

- I will spend time with people, and I will find meaning in being a part of their lives. We will build things together. We will build lives that are integrated.
- I will be full-fledged eccentric by then but still modern and not buying anything at Cracker Barrel.
- I will still be writing, whether or not it brings in money. Still want to write. Books, music. Silly things.
- I will learn how to really play the piano, and I will be playing jazz tunes on my baby grand by candlelight.
- I will have a golden retriever who is boat-savvy.
- I will have some friends who like boating and cramped spaces and who are not allergic to dogs. And who don't pick their nails.
- I will be an accomplished chef. People will want to go vegetarian after they taste my cooking.
- I will still be working but only doing the things I want to do, when I want to do them. Work, but on my terms.

Work gives me meaning. But what about my work gives me meaning? What aspect of it do I want to carry over through the decades?

What would I do if I could do anything I wanted? For as long as I wanted to?

- I will be involved in some charitable cause.
- My life will be lived from my faith outward, and it will be a life that extends grace.
- I will be a better person.
- I will worry less.

• • •

Last night on the way out to my car from grocery shopping, I habitually interlaced my car keys between my fingers. I'm in the retirement mecca for all semi-wealthy senior citizens, and I'm readying myself for attack. Unbelievable.

Truly, the only danger I've faced here has been when I walk past the first six parking spaces closest to the store. They're reserved for the handicapped and official card-carrying Social Security recipients. They're always filled with big, fat, gas-guzzling cars parked slightly askew as if they were being used as part of a heist.

Folklore has it that women go to the bathroom in twos. Well, retired people go to the store in twos—and with good reason. People shrink as they get older. Seeing over the steering wheel becomes an issue. That, along with limited neck mobility (which I have myself, at least once a week), makes depth perception a high-risk activity. Copilots are indispensable—hence, the two-driver technique.

From what I've observed, the role of driver—although stressful—comes with its perks. The driver gets to remain in the car, idling, while the other goes in. In and out in no time. Life is short. They've got better things to do than park correctly and peruse the aisles in tandem for Rolaids.

Generally, I'm in a hurry, too, in these situations—although my reasons elude me. And while I remembered to equip myself against retired muggers from Michigan last night, I managed to forget my wallet in the process. I left it in the basket outside the store.

Upon realizing it, I had visions of my next AMEX statement: a shopping spree at Wal-Mart replete with a case of BenGay and UV-blocker wraparound sunglasses, topped off by a lovely dinner at Shoney's.

I drove back to the store, and the wallet had been turned in—even still had my twenty in it.

All the way home, I chastised myself for my constant state of distraction. I was thinking about a million other things as I loaded groceries into my trunk. My hands placed plastic bags upright while my mind considered how I still needed some protein powder from GNC, needed to call my parents, and I wondered if it were too late in the evening to eat something with chocolate in it.

Until recently, I thought I was good at multitasking. I could scramble eggs, carry on a business conversation, and surf the Net— all at the same time. All proficiently, so I thought.

I think I'm on overload. No wonder I forgot my wallet.

*   *   *

"Dreams" were a walk in the park compared to what I tried to write this morning: my "Reality" version of the thirty-year plan.

The fact that I just sat there and stared at a blank page for about an hour made me feel like a big waste. My career is thriving. I love what I do, but the truth is that I won't be doing it forever. As I drew muscle-bound men with bushy eyebrows in caricature, I realized that I just thought things would naturally unfold and I would fall into the "next step." Letting life "happen." That's kind of what I've been doing lately. I don't think I've always been this way, but I guess somewhere along the way, I got tired or became an "unbeliever"— in me, in how things can change or unfold if I plan and pursue. And although I believe that God does at times engineer natural "fits" and unimpeded "segues," I think ultimately we are responsible to "keep moving" and try doors.

Maybe I see it that way because it's all I can do to just keep moving some days. I've got to believe He has the plan in hand and is just looking for my enthusiasm and cooperation.

That's what I believe on good days, anyway, when I have confidence and don't feel a thousand pressing tasks breathing down my neck. I'm working at believing it through all things. I'm working at it right now as I finish drawing one particularly hideous big-nostriled poor soul with crazed eyes, mouth agape, exposing his fibrillating punching bag thingy. I fill in two tiny strands of hair right above his Dumbo ears and have a fleeting thought about my psyche and what doodling tells about a person. I quickly vow to destroy the paper and keep my bizarre "cartoon people" to myself. I've already got enough to deal with.

All this scrutinizing has turned on a tape of the "should've" fears. I *should've* done more, I *should've* been more. The second-guessing starts with the present and trails back to the first career advice I ever received. It was from my father.

"Get in with a good company that has a good retirement plan." Something I obviously didn't do, as I'm self-employed. "Get good health benefits."

All of this reminds me of a conversation I had with Dad one year. He lodged his formal concern, as he does once a decade now, out on the back porch of his house in North Carolina. He had the "conspiratorial" tone that day, keeping his voice down so as not to alarm my mother, who is always sitting just inside the door as we have the "father-daughter talk." In the distance, creek wildlife chattered away as we sat looking at his boat gently lapping in Dawson's Creek.

"Tell me, Marge, do ya get . . . you know . . . get your . . . ?"

He gestured with both hands as if he were holding a personal pair of healthy-sized breasts, cupping underneath with a bounce— as though he were judging their weight.

I recognized the move and relieved him of the question.

"Yes, Dad, I get my bosoms checked regularly." ("Bosoms" being the acceptable term in our household.)

"Good. Ya know you've got to keep that up," he said nonchalantly, never looking my way.

"I know, Dad."

"And insurance? You've got good health benefits? Enough coverage? Life insurance too? Well, you know, enough to cover the cost of a box and the funeral?" He looked at me this time, arms crossed against his muscular chest.

"Yes, Dad, I am fully covered. And I get regular checkups too." It was an extra-credit answer.

"Good. Good."

I'm not sure if he believed me, but it was a stopping point.

We stared at the renegade squirrel pillaging the bird feeder. It lithely maneuvered through the maze of booby traps my father erected to prevent it from stealing the seeds. A very complicated setup, wire brush affixed upside down across the wood spine that dangles the feeder, grease on the string leading down to it, a makeshift tin roof/skirt that was also greased, set atop it—all to thwart this one squirrel.

Didn't seem to stop him.

"That squirrel! I've tried everything to get him offa there. Can't beat him!"

The feeder looked like a war zone. We watched the squirrel make a mockery of Dad's invention. The time passed, and my father resigned himself to his next fatherly duty, although it was uncomfortable for him. He didn't want to hurt me. He cleared his throat, studying the squirrel.

"Ya know, you're not married—and you're not getting any younger."

I suppressed a laugh—not because it's funny but because of the way he laid it right out there as if, in a purely semantic sense, it were something I'd never considered before, as though it could possibly be late-breaking news to me.

I chuckled and turned my body to face him, shaking my head with a smile. "Yes, Dad, I am aware of that."

"Well, it's just that, well who's gonna take care of you when you're old? Have you considered that?" There was a slight pause, and then he added as an afterthought, "You know, we won't be around then, your mother and me."

It was sweet and it broke my heart. But I stayed focused on the question. Being alone, forever and ever, and old—without anyone. Had I considered that? Hmmm. Just about every sleepless night I've ever spent brings with it those thoughts and that question.

I've come to a rocky stand-down with the marriage thing. I've lived long enough to see marriages flourish and crash, requiring everything of everybody involved. My parents are one of the former, heading toward fifty-five years. It seemed to me, as I looked on, that the principle of iron sharpening iron was heavily in play in marriage. My parents were becoming much more like one another, in the good ways, as time wore on. It's been a reminder of God's ultimate purpose for us all: to create His character in our soul. He uses any tools He can find—whether a spouse or an empty house—and has His way finally, and repeatedly in one area if need be. Nobody is exempt. Nobody gets an easier ride because of the chosen "refinement tool." It can all be difficult at times.

And I have even begun to come to terms with the "getting old" part, but the latter question—the "who's gonna take care of me when I am old?" one—well, that's still a little troll that hides under secure thoughts, lying in wait to scare me half to death.

I don't want my dad to worry for me, as much as I think he likes to sometimes. I cleared my throat and delivered my best "incredulous" tone: "Dad, I am very aware that I am not married. And I am also very aware that I am not getting any younger. And quite frankly, I don't know who will take care of me when I am old, but I am not going to make any long-term relational decisions based on a possible short-term need.

"And I have investments, too, Dad, to take care of myself. I am thinking along those lines."

I must've had a rash when I finished. I was most certainly out of breath and my eyes may have had a crazed look to them. He'd lobbed a legitimate bomb into my camp, and I yelped. All the times we'd ever talked, I'd never come so close to insubordination. And hanging there after my monologue, I was painfully aware of my precarious position. I hoped I hadn't hurt him. He was, after all, just doing what love would dictate.

While my hand was still frozen in its final gesture, he looked into my eyes intensely. "You know who you remind me of?" he asked.

Not at all sure where this was going but grateful for the change of subject, I answered, "No, Dad," my hand still held in the reasoning position.

"That girl—the one on *Seinfeld*—you know the one. What's her name? You know—she's fiery—like you!"

"Elaine, Dad?"

"Yeah, yeah—that's it! Elaine. Aw, you're just like her!" He chuckled and settled back into the wicker chair.

I put my hand down and settled back too. Truth was that he was right—on all counts, especially in relationships. I had to have an alternate plan if the traditional setup didn't happen. I needed to consider relationships responsibly, with care. I needed to have a game plan for them. They are really key in the "Wildest Dreams" planning. In fact, looking over my life stories reveals that the dreams I have written for myself center on a sense of belonging, a network of people who, according to my own future eye, I feel comfortable with. And not just comfortable, but known—and knowing.

These are things I consider as I see my future. I need love. I need forgiveness. I need kindness. I need humor. I need to belong. And I need to be able to give those things to others. That is what makes me feel alive.

Ten, twenty, forty years from now, who will be embarrassed to see my mouth fully open as I laugh at the restaurant? Who will watch my future dog? Who will eat my cooking?

Are these people already in my life, in one shape or form? And if not, how do I invite them in to stay?

Chapter Nine

My Life Stories—
Part 3

The tide pulled back this morning, fully uncovering a beautiful piece of driftwood that I've been admiring since the day I got here. It's large, an old log or tree half-buried in the surf. The part that is exposed is about two feet long with a protruding limb that masquerades as a handle. I've tugged on it more than once in an effort to drag it ashore, but it's mocked me with its immovability.

I'm having another go at it, playing tag with the surf. It goes out—I move in and pull. It comes in—I skitter away. I run up and back like that until I am winded and near surrender.

I've been tugging at the idea of relationships for a few days as well, considering how to address the dilemma I have unearthed. Yesterday, staring at my sketchpad, blue marker in hand, I started to write out what I perceive my relational needs to be:

> *Emotional Intimacy*
> *Sense of Belonging*
> *Sense of Family*

Physical Intimacy
Safety Net

Squinting through my magnifying-glass monocle at the shaky blue letters, I easily saw that I could boil down all my relational needs to the desire to be known fully and the privilege of belonging to something bigger than myself, something meaningful.

The tide is creeping up toward my sneakers. Rubbing my temples hard as I huddle over a hermit crab hole, I chuckle. I am obviously so simple. Two basic needs in my relationships. Funny how unintimidating it is when you put it like that. It's navigable.

Sometimes there are themes, experiences that have no particular overt meaning, that have surpassed the "delete" process of years. Like a distant dream or future déjà vu, they keep coming to remembrance. One of my experiences took place many years ago at a Wednesday night church service on Long Island. There was a guest speaker. Turned out, in a way, the word *speaker* was a bit off. This man was from India, and he gave the entire heated presentation in his native tongue. The only English he employed he used as a punctuation, a stopping point, a reprieve from his red-faced exhortations. His one English phrase was simple: "He will do it! He will do it!" For an hour or more, he paced from the left side of the room to the right, staring each of us in the eye, pointing his finger with each impeccably formed word. *He. Will. Do. It.*

Something miraculous took place, something completely unexpected. After a while, with each repetition, the words began to have life, and the life in those words began to feed me. I began to believe that He *would* do it. I made the leap to that lovely childlike trust of believing in impossibilities. *He would do it.*

The phrase is echoing in my mind as I get up and walk east toward the huge heron in the distant surf. Maybe, just maybe, He will do it—or maybe He *is already* doing it and I am just blind to it.

Pinching my chin in the zipper of my jacket, I bundle up and lean into the wind.

I don't even know what "it" fully is. I'm just sure that I know He can do "it."

• • •

These snowbird ladies from Michigan are shaming me. As I jog by in rags and pilly sweaters, they glide by me in matching everything, perfectly done nails and, apparently, the one thing that any self-respecting retired lady should never leave the house without: ruby red lipstick. Most of them have no other makeup on at that hour, but I have not seen one woman without her ruby red lips on. I pray to God that is a thing that naturally happens to women and not another thing I will have to add to my list of goals: "Wear lipstick at all times. Gradually move toward darker red shades as needed."

Duly inspired this morning, I tackled my vision of life forty years from now.

My Life Stories
Wildest Dreams Version
Forty Years from Now
- I will finally be who I am in my soul. I think this will be my best time in life. I'm pretty sure I was born to be old.
- I will be healthy. I will always draw attention to the fact that I have all my own teeth.
- I will still be living as I was at the thirty-year mark, but I may cut down on the beach jogging. I could break a hip.
- I won't allow my hair to get that bluish tint to it.

Gotta stay close to my colorist. Wonder what her forty-year plan is.

- I will be at my wisdom peak. In fact, people will know me as being "wise."
- I won't talk a lot. Wise people never do.
- Friends, friends, friends. Surrounded by friends.
- If I've never been married, I may downgrade my criteria—just to give it a try.

Fifty Years from Now and Beyond

- I just don't want to be in a "home."
- I want to retain control of my bowels.
- If they still let me, I'll drive an old convertible. Whatever wrinkles I am destined to get will surely be on me already. Sun exposure won't matter.
- People, as many as I can stand, all around me—most of the time.
- I may take in other senior citizens as roommates, like on *The Golden Girls.*
- I'll be a grand hostess, and when people step foot in my house, it won't have that "old lady" smell. In fact, I vow that I *personally* will not get that "old lady" smell.

   I gotta keep taking showers every day and not hoard old newspapers and mementos. I think that's how you get that smell.

- I won't wear any toiletries that smell like lilac, or anything too powdery.

   I wonder if my money will last this long.
   (What money?)

- I may be working part-time as a waitress at Bob's Big Boy, dispensing eggs and wisdom.

- I will have taken up painting, and my work will be psychedelic.

* * *

Took a hard look at my teeth in the mirror on my way out of the bathroom this morning. Didn't know that *not* getting gingivitis was such a life goal for me.

There's a sheath of seaweed about the size of a place mat that keeps washing up on the sand. It is luminescent green. I've heard that the Gulf gets its emerald glow from that seaweed. Up and back. Up and back. The surf folds it and unfolds it. Twists it up like a rag and spreads it out again. It's slowly drifting east to Panama City with each wave. It has no choice. It's all just kind of happening to it.

Just finished reading through my "Wildest Dreams" life stories. There's no particular rhyme or reason to them. But patterns are emerging. There are a lot of things I didn't know about me, like how I've been drifting to Panama City.

Twenty Years from Now
This will be the easiest because I've got all the pieces now.
- I will be in early retirement but still working at what I want to do.
- Writing, writing. Speaking, singing.
- I may be caring for my parents in my home with assistance.

More money. Bigger house.

Pretty much the same as the ten-year plan, except less of it. The same as the thirty-year plan, except building proactively toward it.

I may even get a face-lift if they learn how to do it without giving you that "surprised" look.

● ● ●

Took my afternoon walk. Passed what looked like the TV models for PoliGrip and Aleve: the perfect retired couple. He with a full head of white hair, golf tan, fit, and his wife still trim in her perfectly rolled jeans and starched white shirt, with her own impressive head of shoulder-length gray hair pulled back in a neat ponytail.

Behind them, in an uneven train, followed their grown children with spouses and kids and dogs. It was the perfect setting. The perfect extended family. The relational dynamic was evident, even from a distance. Their postures, the gesturing, the tone of their voices, were that of friends, old and dear friends spending a vacation together. It's sweet to see that.

And sad, because there was no escaping the honest truth: I'd been a poor friend to my own parents for most of my adult life, partially because I wasn't prepared for the shift from child to friend, and partially because I just wasn't paying enough attention.

To be called a true friend by my parents—what could be more wonderful? And what better way to become a friend than by *being* there, seeing their needs and helping?

And the needs are there. That's the tragic oversight I allowed. My parents—though not feeble by any means—are moving forward into a time where they do have needs. Up until now, that time has seemed like another country, with no map to help me traverse the gap. But there *is* a way to span it, a nearly imperceptible bridge that serves to assist in the role reversal from "needer" to "supporter." It's so easy to miss and so easy to avoid because the signs that denote its presence are bread crumbs in the forest. If you're not watching intently, they will be gobbled up by any number of things, gone without a trace.

Those crumbs are the slight changes, changes reminiscent of grandparents, like a father welcoming help instead of resisting it, or taking advice rather than giving it. The truth of the change seems so unnatural at first. You're sure you've misinterpreted or misread a cue, yet the next concession comes, then the next, and it feels as if time itself is pushing you from behind—unwillingly—toward the bridge. You go—unprepared, unceremoniously, probably much like the way parents begin with their babies—compelled by a bundle of living need but without an "owner's manual."

For a few years now I've been making the crossing blindly, without forethought. I was missing its scope and importance. That journey, marked by its subtle but unmistakable cues, is from child to friend. From taker to giver. In our society, where we laud youth and shame the natural fate of aging, I think we ultimately lose something else of great value: the permission to progress in our own passages, our own aging process. And perhaps the greater loss: the ensuing peace that comes through participating in the aging of those we've known the longest.

I was missing it until recently. My parents *are* getting older. Our time *does* have a visible end. A phone call is not nearly as good as a visit.

And being a daughter or son does not automatically qualify you to be a friend. Friendship requires trust. Trust requires faith. Faith requires belief. And I think that on some level, belief begins with an invitation.

This next year, I want to extend the invitation to my parents, through any number of delicate signals we all will recognize and understand. I want them to believe, believe that I *want* to be a friend; to have faith, faith that I *can* be a friend; and to trust, trust that I *will* be a *good* friend, if welcomed in.

I need to press a little harder in conversation. Listen more. Give things not asked of me. Nothing big; only tiny steps. Little inroads and tests that could possibly result in small progressions, mutual signals and acceptances passing between us like secret handshakes. I believe that time and persistence will weave together to form a safety net that my parents will recognize—if they want to, if I put in the effort.

My journey from dependent to friend will be arduous at times, I'm sure. But honestly, to have the opportunity to make that journey while we are all still here—that is prize enough all in itself.

Chapter Ten

Overlooked Provisions

I know some people who hear from God all the time. It's like they've tapped into some hotline or something. I envy them. I am still on cans and string if frequency of communication is any measure. It takes a lot to get through to me, and this retreat is no exception.

I hardly ever get a "direct" word from on high. Mostly it is just an overall "sense" of things that cause me to move in a certain direction, which is either affirmed or thwarted according to its accuracy. Some would call that conviction or "leading." I wouldn't dare put a title to it for fear of glorifying the wrong thing and causing others to fend for themselves in my primitive world. Unique to me maybe, but effective over the years and as recently as this morning, when after one of my top five prayers—*Lord, help me to see what I need to see*—I had one of those overarching "sense" moments. It was about my need to be known and God's provision for it.

> Before I formed you in the womb I knew you,
> before you were born I set you apart.[10]

I have made it a habit to memorize Scripture right before falling asleep and when I run. Some of those passages I've made into rhythmic chants that mimic my cadence. This morning as I ran in the rain, that one came back to me, and a little part of the riddle found rest.

In a purely spiritual sense, I *am* known. In the most intimate sense of the word *know*, I *am* known and have been since before I took my first breath. God's response to my cry to "be known" is that *He does.* He knows me. He knows me better than I could ever know myself. And, of course, God—knowing the realist that I am—knows I need to understand how this all plays out in my life, like where the "legs" are on these concepts.

After forty-five minutes of off-kilter jogging in uneven sand, I plopped down on a sheared ledge at the shoreline. The tide was fully in, and the ledge I settled on was stately but not strong. It was formed only last night. I poked holes in the crispy upper layer as I had my next primal epiphany: God was already attempting to meet my relational needs – I just wasn't letting Him.

Names, situations, attempts for relationship that I spurned or—worse yet—dismissed presented themselves like witnesses at a trial. There were people already in my life who were part of God's provision for me, yet I did not have eyes to see them because they were not presenting themselves in a form I expected.

I expected.

I expected the answer to my needs to come in the form of one person, a husband, who would bring an extended family. One relationship, one man to fill all my needs? And in the meantime, while I am waiting on *whatever,* I am not recognizing or receiving God's provision in these areas.

The church in Acts came to mind. People—as in *plural*—providing for *people.* Community. Bound together by circumstance perhaps—something we view as a detriment in this day and age, a weakness almost. We are raised to be emancipated, to seclude ourselves from one another in order to limit our exposure to one another. I wonder if it is a thinly veiled attempt to escape the "iron sharpening iron" process that occurs naturally when, due to mutual dependence or survival, you can't just walk out the door. This expectation of striking out on one's own can be destructive to community, both familial and extended.

It's a shame we don't live more centrically, with our families closer in. We need their wisdom and their "knowing"—the sense of being known by someone who has known us all our lives. And that is just the obvious example. Most of us don't have our grandparents, our extended family near us. That is the fact, but then there is the promise: that God will set the solitary in families. Fact or promise?

The promise is what I mull over as I slide down the front of the cliff to walk the moist edge of the receding tide. My feet sink deep as I remember people like Keith, who commandeered me off the subway in New York after church one afternoon. There at the station's descending entry, he grabbed my arm for at least the fourth Sunday in a row, imploring me, locking my eyes through his thick horn-rimmed glasses.

"Margaret, we absolutely will *not* take no for an answer this week. You will come and stay the afternoon and, if need be, the night with us. This is what "church" *is*: family!"

Off I went with him, back up to Harlem, where his wife, Rita, and their two children were already sprawled out on their tiny apartment floor surrounded by *The New York Times* and coloring books in radiant sunlit patches. Soup was on the stove, and classical music played in the background. I stayed there most of the day, doing what families do—talking, resting, watching television I probably would never watch alone—intermittently bored and comforted. But that's what relationship is to some degree, isn't it? It's not all *go-go-go!* or *whooo-who!!* It was the first of many comforting/ familial —as in God's community—afternoons I would spend with that family.

That was God's provision for me—to be set in a family. To belong. To be known. I didn't take it seriously enough.

Halfway back to the Howard, the parade of overlooked provisions continues. There are names and opportunities and open doors I so insensitively pushed shut because *I didn't see it* as God's provision. It didn't look like what I was expecting.

Almost home, on stair number three, my guilt trip is a bit assuaged when I realize that better women than myself had made the same mistakes, and those mistakes were now the parables of generations. Like Mary and Martha, when they expected Jesus to come to their house.[11] They both were believing that Jesus—their friend and the Son of God—would show up. But there was a difference in their expectation of *how* He would show up. Mary recognized Him—the provision of His presence, the provision *in* Him—immediately when He arrived, and she stopped everything—including "preparing" the house for Him—to enjoy, experience, and learn from Him.

But as it would be for any one of us if someone that important were expected at our house, there were certain "preparations" to be made, certain "tasks" to complete, and *then* God—His presence—would have the correct, conducive environment to show up. Martha didn't recognize that He had already shown up despite where she was in her own preparation for Him. Despite Martha's conscientious efforts, Jesus bypassed the "traditions," the expectations that could possibly confuse the "expectant" Martha. Traditions or relationship? Law or love? My adherence or God's benevolence? Which is it? Do we control God by doing things "just so"? Can we make Him like us any better by doing it all "this way" or "that"?

Jesus spent most of His life here on earth being a breathing testament to never thinking you can figure God—or His systems—out. I am certain He wanted Martha's attention on Him—His living, breathing presence in her immediate moment. I am also as certain He did not want her attentions on practices, social edicts, and "religiosity" instead. She missed God's provision in her own space—not because she was wicked or dull but because she had settled for someone else's definition of how He would come. His words to her sting my own soul: "Martha, Martha . . . you are worried and upset about many things, but only one thing is needed. Mary has chosen what is better, and it will not be taken away from her."[12]

I know I'm not an anarchist—I just don't want to miss God. I don't want to walk along the edge of His order. I don't want to miss Him, because I trust His order more than I trust Him.

So as I peel away my moist paint-spattered holy sweatshirt, I begin prayer number six: *God, help me to see your provision and choose "what is better." Make me a Mary.*

Chapter Eleven

It's About Time

Mary made time. Mary took time. God showed up and Mary sat down. Nothing was as important to Mary as His presence—in the present moment. And for me, it's all adding up to time. How I measure it. How I value it. How I spend it.

The moon is so full and bright tonight that I can see the impressions my steps left in the sand from the house to the shore. Down the beach to my left, I can see two people walking arm in arm. They take their time, with slow swaying paces that remind me of the version of Dido and Aeneas on the Aria record. Robust swells of lush strings, mournful and resolute, with a beauty that pours from the invisible dimension that always remains just out of the range of normal senses. I watch the couple, swathed in powdery silver light, move as one shadow to its beautiful rhythm. I can tell even at this distance that they are elderly.

I am trying to be discreet, but I know that I am staring. I am jealous of their peaceful union. The wind is still, and I hear only silence as they come closer. Peaceful silence—the best gift of all in a long relationship. The ability to leave behind cumbersome words and find absolute comfort in only the nearness of another.

I have a thermos of decaf Starbucks driven into the sand next to me. It's leaning toward the surf. Earlier in my visit here, I know I would have made a bigger effort to center and level it, but as I look at the brushed aluminum cylinder sitting cockeyed in the moonlight, I realize that I just don't care enough to right it. Part of me recognizes this as some form of progress.

I watched television for two days straight this week. Bad, bad seventies television like *Starsky and Hutch*, *McMillan and Wife*, and *The Rockford Files*—anything to distract me from what I just cannot seem to do: finish my "Reality" life stories. After a while, the exercise became futile because without the "wild" dreams, I had no picture of where I would be in ten, five, fifty, or any amount of years.

In fact, if nothing else, this dreaming has shown me that although I've been moving forward in a directed manner in most areas of my life, before now I have not given near enough thought to the sum total of my days and what I hope to accomplish within them.

• • •

The sunrise after the hurricane was by far the most spectacular. It's a metaphor for me right now—after the most horrific storm, a beautiful display of God's wonder, generous, frivolous, and in the midst of disarray.

It's a God-principle—the directed destruction. The refinement that comes from hardship. The correct weights and balances that emerge from true trauma. It's all there. We just don't see it most of the time. But people who are struggling with illness do. It's as if the pyramid of values rights itself somehow when time is clearly marked. It's sobering to see what changes, what falls down the ladder of importance. Life is no longer about the temporal issues, the trivial, like paying down the mortgage or getting that next "thing."

It becomes about living long enough to hold a newborn grandchild or having vision enough to see a furrowed brow grow deeper with age. It's about feeling someone's touch a little bit deeper, and laughing with or without pain.

As I muse, I pull out one of the journals I brought with me and flip back several months. My mother was healing from a fall. I flew to North Carolina to help, to just *be* with her. And I wrote a lot.

Once the dexterous gardener, Mom is moving quite slowly with a walker, hip pinned with steel. Every distance covered is a chore. She doesn't want to move, and I don't blame her.

We've taken our respective places for days now: her tiny frame swallowed up in the recliner, and me, sleepy from the heat, trying to remain upright on the couch. We've gone from the History Channel, to romance, to Turner Classics. Despite the pain medication, she can name every obscure actress and theme.

I watch her sleep on and off. Sometimes when I wake, I catch her watching me too. I wonder what she's thinking, though I'm too timid to ask. I'm not sure that I want to know. After all, she has power over me. Always has.

All week I've been encouraging her to move, tempting her with a fresh-air visit on the back porch. Dawson's Creek is just beyond the lawn. It's a little tributary framed by the tullie reeds. Wild ducks, heron, and even owls nest just beyond the length of the small dock that my father and two bona fide, part-time gospel preachers built when he first arrived here. My father talks of the experience still.

"They worked like dogs for me. In ninety-degree heat. Never complained."

It really made an impression on him, because from that day forward, he returned the kindness by volunteering as a pallbearer at their humble church funerals.

"I tell you, Margaret, they don't hold back at these country

funerals. The pastor and all the folks in the congregation sing their eulogies, and they tell the truth—not like at other funerals, where you know people are lying through their teeth. They do it like (he says, as he performs his best gospel rendition, miming sweat and fire), 'Brother James was a mighty man!' And then the rest of the group says in all different ways, 'That's right!,' 'Um-hm!' 'You know that's true!'

" 'Now he loooved his car a little too much.'

" 'Uh-huh.'

" 'And he wasn't the most faithful man . . .'

" 'AA-men!'

" 'But his heart was good—his heart was good.'

" 'Yeas, yeas.' "

My father would return from these gatherings red-faced and wet through his suit jacket, always moved in ways he admits he can scarcely explain. He'd entertain my mother with his imitations, which she'd counter with astonished exclamations like, "Really?"

It's the kind of camaraderie that's held my parents together for over fifty years. Genuine friendship. Respect. Discipline and mutual interests, like the creek and the birds and the cycles of life passing through their backyard over seasons.

I know it will do her good to see these things outside, remind her of what is true. I want her to lose herself in wild lives for a moment. She can name species, migrating habits, quirky little facts like who eats their young and who leaves them behind, always with that wry Irish grin as if I should take heed myself. Perhaps such mysteries lie in her too.

It takes almost the entire week, but I finally get her to go the twenty paces with me. It's only fifteen feet, but it might as well be fifteen miles. For her, it is laborious.

I settle her into her favorite wicker chair, and it creaks as she shifts to find the perfect ladylike position. Beyond the thin screen, the world carries on. We talk a little about it and then are still, silently observing.

I am fully there. I am nowhere else. In fact, the energy of the moment with my mother fills me with such emotion, it feels as though my ribcage is elevated, like I've swallowed a balloon. The "presence" of it all is so close to the skin that it is almost painful— she and I, breathing together, looking out over the creek.

I turn toward her after a time and reach for her hand. It is a risk. We haven't held hands since I was a child, and even then her grasp mostly served as a towrope to hurry me across the city street.

As I take her left hand in my right, she smiles slightly. She understands, I think, what I am feeling. I hold her hand in mine and treasure the warmth of it. We stay that way for about five minutes, when she abruptly turns to face me. She has that intense mother look as she stares deeply into me. Inside, I feel an unexpected leap. I recognize the look. It is the "I am your mother and I am about to tell you the secret of life" look. It's the comment you wait for your whole life, the one bit of motherly guidance you just know will come one day and change your life irrevocably.

I match her stare with anticipation. Slowly, her mouth opens and the words come with intent and deep recognition: "You have my nose." It's all she says. Then she turns back to the creek.

I am shocked—and initially a little disappointed. Her nose? Is that a metaphor or something? Her nose?

I scramble for a few seconds before I realize it's perfect—all of it. I have her nose. That is the truth. Perhaps she infers other things, like I have her heart and I have her values and I have her goodness and maybe her pigeon-toed gait. Or maybe it just means that I have her nose.

*What could be more wonderful, more meaningful, than that?
To feel the warmth of your mother's hand on a mild spring day. To
look out over a beautiful vista together in silence. To be connected
by the stare of love that only a mother can give. To have the eyes to
recognize the entire gift unwrapping, the senses to know its depth
and significance, the time to enjoy its unfolding.*

*Somewhere in another dimension, I'm sure there was the
sound of a purposeful "click." One line lowering into place, another
lowering to connect with it, truth fusing with truth, spirit to spirit
and life to life, creating a momentary circuit to something greater
than words can embody, something much higher than imaginations
can reach.*

*It is said that we use only 10 percent of our brain. I wonder if
it is true of the heart, because as that circuit conducts that moment,
I feel my heart gorge with life, and I feel things I didn't know I
could.*

●　●　●

I've noticed more than once that people who are gravely ill have
clear sight. They see what the true concerns are. They let the rest
drip off their lives, unable or unwilling to expend energy on such
petty things. The true concern becomes qualitative, not quantita-
tive. It's the quality of what is before them, not how much or how
long. And again, all of that boils down to time.

And that is the key to the "fullness of joy." You can't experience
it in the past. That's already over. Gone. You can't experience it in
the future. You can *hope* to experience it then. There is only one
place to experience it—it is in *the present moment.*

Is it any wonder that the present moment is the very thing
under siege in my life—in our culture? *Do more, be more, stay more*

connected, accomplish five things at the same time—don't waste time!
That is the mantra of our entire economy. Get the consumer to
want enough to purchase, to churn the financial exchange. It's all
about appealing to our rudimentary human appetites: the lust of
the eyes, the lust of the flesh, and the pride of life.

I'm not against it. In and of itself it is innocuous. But when it
becomes part of our value system—whether by invitation, adop-
tion, or purely osmosis—it's wrong. It's off-kilter—"off the mark."
That makes it sin.

Accomplish more, make more, get more, "be" more. It's all led
to strange truths we Americans take for granted now, like people
needing storage units because they have so much stuff that they
can't fit it in their house, where they—a solitary family unit—live!
The rest of the world huddles together, and we need more room for
things we obviously don't need every day. And even more insulting
are our latest rude practices. Like how did the person who is calling
on the cell phone become more important than the person who
cared to show up, the person across the table or seated next to you
patiently and awkwardly waiting? And so many other things, like
typing and talking on the phone at the same time and needing five
different ways to be contacted. Maybe we were never meant to be
that accessible. Maybe what doesn't get done or addressed can truly
wait. Is anything really *that* critical?

Time. We are being robbed blind of it, and it's happening right
underneath our noses, with our permission.

We were built to work, and we were designed to rest. It's a cycle
of expenditure and refueling. It's biblical. It's called Sabbath. Why
is it so difficult to maintain Sabbath? Not a "day," but an attitude
of protection concerning the usage of time.

Our ability to change is limited to the present moment. We can
only affect *this* moment and hope it affects all the others. We can

experience and live and feel only in the present moment—in this unit of time. It's all we have here on earth, ultimately, no matter what we base our life on.

In thy presence is fullness of joy.

If only I can learn to *be* more in the present moment, I believe I will experience the presence of God more fully in the small, mundane tasks and pauses of the day.

I need to slow down and take Him in more.

Chapter Twelve

Breaking Protocol

I'm having a lovely dinner on a stormy night. The table is set and candles are flickering across the house. There's a fire in the hearth. Rain slips down the back side of the house in windy streaks, blurring the moonlit shoreline.

I'm staring at my food and imagining how my friends would deride me. They would never deem tofu "lovely."

I've been a vegetarian for over twenty years now—not because I have some great conviction about it but because ever since I discovered where meat came from, I have been repulsed by it.

It was a fateful day one autumn when my mother and I drove by Volbracht's dairy farm. Per habit, we scanned the field to see "what the cows were up to." The farm was uncharacteristically empty. I asked where all the cows were. My mother, in her typical attempt to glean every opportunity for a lesson, informed me it was their supper time. She pointed to a tiny lone shack not nearly big enough for even one cow, where she claimed the cows were busy clearing the table and washing their dinner dishes.

I was fascinated at the thought: Cows washing dishes. I saw the cows in my mind, some sitting contentedly around the table, some balancing their massive bodies on two spindly hind legs as they bent over the huge trough sink, scrubbing away in aprons.

The thought made some sort of cosmic connection and led me to ask the ill-fated question, "Where does hamburger come from?"

My mother's panic was plain to see. There was a long silence as the farm faded from view out the passenger-side window. I tried to picture hamburger on a tree like an apple or in the ground like a carrot, but nothing seemed right.

"Well, M, it comes from a cow," she finally offered. Brilliant the way she didn't quite lie but didn't give the full picture.

I toyed with the image of hamburgers coming out of the same openings that milk came out of. That didn't seem right. I had to ask. "Like the milk does?"

The explanation that followed sparked a horrifying conversation that ended later that night when the mystery of meat was fully unearthed and my mother had had enough of my intrusive, guilt-inducing questions. I believe the final blow was right after our Shake 'N Bake dinner, as we cleaned up.

"Mom, what about chicken?" I half pleaded, holding out hope that perhaps it wasn't the same fate that befell the rest of my barnyard favorites.

"Chicken comes from chicken, Margaret. And the good Lord gave them all to us to eat. Don't despise His gifts," she huffed in frustration.

I knew that I was over my question limit. I had the clear picture now. From then on, I tried to hide all my meat under my mashed potatoes, along with the dreaded peas.

Hidden along there with them was a message, a subtle one that most little girls got at that time: "Don't rock the boat. Be accommodating and nice to others." I know it was well meant, but the translation is, "Personal choice is another way to make others feel uncomfortable, and it's unladylike to make others uncomfortable."

I think about that for a moment as I stir-fry ginger root. *Why have I allowed that?* As the shavings become opaque, I realize that my experience of religion has driven that attitude even deeper. And worse yet, I think I have only myself to blame.

There's a world of difference between living Christlike kindness and accommodating everyone else to the point of losing sight of what Christ's individual calling is for me. Somehow, I've managed to put all the great, loving concepts into a ball of "non-choice." I think I've even assigned it merit, like it makes me more godly if I am liked because I don't divert or assert.

But even Christ Himself was unaccomodating at times—to the people who tried to snare Him in His own ancient laws, to the religious and the self-righteous, and even to His own beloved disciples—*if* the result of acquiescing was not conducive to fulfilling His understanding of what His calling and purpose was. And so much of His purpose was related to people—loving people. It's such a messy juxtaposition in many ways. Love people by not accommodating people—all perfectly in His case.

I ponder the subtle, overlooked theme woven throughout the many accounts of Him. He was a divinely inspired individualist. He was a radical. He chose loving people over pleasing the "powers that be." He chose to confound the expectations of the hierarchy, the part of society that took pride in "knowing" God and His protocol. The prostitute washing His feet with her tears—how repulsive that was to the "holy" folks who were present. When Simon questioned Christ about it, His response was so cutting, so blunt: "See this woman? I came into your house. You gave me no water for my feet, but *she* has washed my feet with her tears and wiped them with the hairs of her head. You gave me no kiss, but since I came, she has not ceased to kiss my feet."[13] Jesus' response was meant to show Simon that, unbeknownst to himself, he did not love God, for if he had, he would have done not only what was expected of him—the oversights Jesus cited—but much more, as Mary did. In this and so many other examples like it, Jesus broke with tradition to influence, to love, to serve a person, not the limited expectations of a few.

I am certain Christ did this to remind the "holy" folks that *He alone* is God and He can break His own rules as well as uphold them—and even gradate them, as in His choice for the greatest: "Love the Lord your God with all your heart, soul, mind, and body. Love your neighbor as yourself."[14]

I'm so thankful there's nothing in there about chicken.

My tofu duly seasoned and cooked, I move toward the dining room. I chuckle, remembering my mother's last-ditch effort to change the subject by adding "You'll hurt His feelings!" to the "Don't despise the Lord's gift" statement. Although I am certain that I've hurt God's feelings more than I could number, I'm sure He doesn't mind if I don't eat His peas.

*   *   *

I never close the shades here, as that would thwart the purpose for which I came. I hate being cut off from the Gulf. So tonight, I lay wide awake in the powdery moonlight, willing myself to sleep, as I knew I'd need to be up at 3:00 a.m. to make a flight for a dear friend's wedding. It was the only engagement I'd allowed on my month's calendar.

Over my years of travel, I have written a book in my mind. It is titled *Inverse Rules of Travel.* It includes truths like "The shorter amount of time you have, the nicer the hotel you will stay in" and "You only need Advil when you can't possibly get any." Tonight illustrated another key principle: "The earlier you must wake, the harder it will be to get to sleep."

I went to bed early, using all my usual sleep techniques but with no luck. I added Nytol, even turned up the heat, pulled the covers over my head. Nothing. My last resort was reading by candlelight, hoping that by exhausting my eyes I would exhaust my body. It worked. Just about four pages from the end of the novel, I began to feel sleepy.

I reached over the candle to place the book on the nightstand, keeping my eyes half closed so I wouldn't wake up again. Finally exhausted, I lay back down.

Within minutes, I was unusually warm. *Maybe the Nytol is kicking in*, I thought. Through my eyelids, I made out flashes of approaching thunder. Flares that seemed as close as the foot of my bed rose so bright that I had to force my eyes open to take a look. When I did, I beheld another first: my own terrycloth robe burning. My arm—the arm that reached over the candle—was on fire.

Wide awake now, I threw myself down on the antique Persian rug and rolled—rolled and imagined the headlines: "Singer emulsifies self in apparent attempt to find peace. Excerpts from bizarre sketchpad and journal enclosed." And "Loving the afterlife to death—today on *Montel.*"

How calm I felt inside with the thought of perishing, only begrudging entry into urban folklore. I rolled and also calculated. *Did I have enough money to pay for the rug once I'd destroyed it, should I survive?* I know I was screaming too. But not like someone who might be facing death—more like someone chastising herself for her stupidity.

The fire went out. And when I turned on every light in the house, I saw that not a mark was on anything—including my robe. I smoothed out my robe and my hair, turning around in place as if there might be a hidden witness to my debacle. Through my panicked breaths, the ultimate humor of it rose, and I laughed hard and long. By then it was 1:15 a.m. and I was ready for anything.

Still, having to sing "Our Father" perfectly for that "perfect day" is no small pressure, so I willed myself to get back in bed and pretended I didn't nearly set the house and myself on fire. I lay that way for a while, stunned and amused, and then the realization jolted me that I had not bothered to check if I lost any hair in the inferno.

I got up and checked my brows. Still there. Checked the hair on the back of my head. Still there. Checked the hair on my arms. A little singed and bare. As I showered, I told myself it wasn't all that bad. Some people pay good money for hairless arms.

Chapter Thirteen

Somewhere Out There

I wandered around the Wal-Mart Supercenter today, looking for nothing in particular, curious about the exact differences of a Supercenter Wal-Mart versus a regular Wal-Mart.

I noticed people staring at me. As I passed the children's section, I caught sight of myself in the mirror. This morning's run had been bone chilling, and I had the bright red windburned face to prove it. I looked like a tourist who had sat in the sun too long.

I wandered the aisles, looking for any signs of "Super-ism." It all looked like the regular Wal-Mart to me. My lobster complexion caught the eye of some young clerk and I seized the moment. Brave to the core now, I asked the question without stuttering, as if it were a pop quiz, "What's the difference between a Super Wal-Mart and a regular Wal-Mart?"

He pointed over my head and to the left. "Groceries, ma'am. Wholesale groceries. You can find pretty much everything you'd ever want over there."

Pretty much anything I'd ever want, I mused. Oh, if only it were true.

I made my way "over there" and happened upon the sample aisle, where delicacies like pigs-in-a-blanket and barbecued pork are offered in tiny Dixie cups to the hungry and iron-bellied. I abstained for the most part—until the fresh chocolate chip cookies. That with the free Hawaiian punch made good wandering food as I walked the aisles.

The urge to buy was strong, until I promised myself to keep my wits and not be seduced by the oversized mutant packages. I have had some mishaps in the past with bulk grocery purchases. Like the A1 Steak Sauce vat that I purchased for $7.95 for my veggie burgers. The whole thing is a great savings, especially if you are prone to buy last minute from a Texaco station like I am. But it took almost a year and a half to get through the bottle, even with barbecues and meat-eating friends. By the end, people were refusing to eat it. Too many botulism possibilities.

Worse yet was the time I was expecting company for Thanksgiving and went to Sam's for toilet paper. The smallest pack they had was practically a full palette. It obscured my view as I pushed the basket to the register. That is how I missed it, the preholiday serpentine line, which cruelly happened to be formed by everyone I'd ever known and had not seen in a long time. As fate would have it, they were all buying respectable things like vegetables and lasagna. I was hard to miss with my mountain of Charmin Extra Soft. Person after person came to me wanting to "catch up," all the while suspiciously eyeing my five-year stash. But no one acknowledged it. The only thing that could've made it worse would've been if I'd had two big buckets of Metamucil sitting atop it.

Although it's economic, buying in bulk is pretty pointless for me. My singleness disqualifies me. I can't consume the smallest portions within the suggested freshness guidelines, but that doesn't prevent me from loitering, mostly in the stationery/office section. This time was no exception. I was once again waylaid in the office gadgets aisle.

The new object of my fascination? A financial calculator. This thing did it all. It would help me track investments and figure out mortgages, just as soon as I read the twenty-two-page instruction booklet on how to operate it. Good enough for me. I bought it and a fat plastic pen that had four different colors in it and spent the better part of the evening perched in front of the fire, trying to read the half-Chinese/half-English instruction manual. The font used in the manual cannot be bigger than five points. I eventually gave up.

· · ·

This morning I turned on my computer for the first time since arriving at the beach. It came stocked with financial software that I never bothered with before. After a bit, I found that Quicken had some easy-to-use financial calculators. I was able to plug in my current numbers: the years until I think I may retire and the rates at which I think my money will grow.

The results? I will be broke. At sixty-five, even.

I paced around the living room, coffee in hand, wondering what I'd been thinking all these years. *Why on earth did I not seriously determine these numbers before? Who did I think was going to do this for me?*

I stared at the mid-morning light streaking the kitchen counter. There, in all its deflated glory, was the answer: last week's Lotto ticket. I buy one perhaps once a year. To me it's an adult version of the twenty-five-cent toy dispensers at grocery stores from which you hope you get the displayed item, but most times you get something inferior. Still, every time I buy a ticket, I actually think there is a chance I could win.

Over a weekend getaway with a few friends one year, I discreetly made my way to the Lotto forms. While standing at the Stop-and-Go kiosk, I felt the presence of someone looking over my shoulder. There stood the rest of the gang, jostling one another for position. Penciling quietly, we sheltered our Lotto forms from one another as if they were grade-school math tests. It was all in fun, but we were halfway serious.

On the way home, we corporately derided ourselves, making the sane argument—the one about not getting our hopes up and knowing that we will never win. And, of course, it concluded with the perpetual sappy conversation that lawsuits are made of—how if any one of us actually did win, we would share the money.

When Sunday came, my friend Carolyn ran out to buy the paper for the winning numbers. Feigning restraint, each of us nonchalantly copied the figures and retreated to our respective corners to compare.

One by one, heavy-sighed responses emerged: "Oh well, guess I'll be working through next year."

"I didn't win—but I got two! I almost won!"

In the Lotto aftermath, a palpable disappointment filled the room, and Carolyn voluntarily confessed first.

"Was it just me, or did any of you think that you would actually win?"

Sheepishly looking around at one another, the sheer ludicrousness of our expectations shamed us all, as evidenced by the nervous giggling. We all thought we were going to win. In fact, Carolyn admitted to feeling sorry for the rest of us because she was positive she would win.

And why? Why did each of us believe that? I asked myself as I rinsed the coffee filter. Because it's a "somewhere out there" possibility that demands a level of trust but resists close scrutiny. You trust that you *could* win. After all, *someone* will. And on an even more pure level, you believe that somewhere in the scheme of things, you will be looked after to the point of not needing to examine whether you are responsible for creating a way for you to be "looked" after.

Maybe it's worse for a single person. Maybe I've always thought that along the way, a husband was going to bisect my life and bring all of these answers with him. In fact, upon closer examination, I think I put off very important financial steps that were critical to my well-being, believing that out there, somewhere, someone would take care of it for me, or that somehow it would all work out without requiring much thought or effort from me.

I began saving for retirement at twenty-seven. I gave the maximum allowable to my IRA every year after that—two thousand dollars—and that seemed like a lot to me. But it was worse than paltry when plugged into the financial calculator. At fifty-five, I would have a whopping $81,677 at a modest rate of growth, which means I could probably live for about four years if I learned to like Dinty Moore beef stew and Ramen noodles and made all my own clothes. And the government, should there still be a Social Security fund, will be happy to contribute another couple hundred dollars a month.

I am not in good shape here.

There is not enough time for me to be lax about this, and I don't have all the know-how to do this for myself. I need to find someone who can help me. I've got to start saving more. And I need to return the calculator. It was a crazy impulse buy.

On the way home, I'll buy another Lotto ticket.

Chapter Fourteen

Humility

What is it about outlet malls that makes me overspend? How is it that I can walk through any mall in the entire U.S. and not be moved to buy a thing, yet I go to the outlets and walk away a few hundred dollars lighter?

I want to meet the marketing mind behind this diabolical concept.

I drove to the Silver Sands Outlet Mall this afternoon just "to take a break," I told myself. Of course, I had no intention of buying. I've always held the belief that outlets are not much cheaper than catching a good sale day at Macy's. In fact, the few times I have gone, the prices have been the same as I've seen in any other store.

I needed something to do, so I went. And bought and bought and bought. Shirts, jeans, hats, and even socks. I couldn't get control. Everything I saw, I thought I needed. Some of it I didn't even bother trying on—not because I was certain of the size but because I had scared myself to death in the dressing room of the first store.

There are three types of mirrors I forbid myself to look into: airplane bathroom mirrors, the ones behind the car sun visor, and the ones in group dressing rooms. I got a little sloppy today at Old

Navy. There I was in the fluorescent lights—bent over trying on a pair of jeans—when out of the corner of my eye, I saw a big white mass. Some stranger's behind. Wearing the same underwear as I was. Same, but surely a few sizes bigger, mimicking my every move, moving in tandem with me. Something about it seemed oh so familiar, and with a cruel jolt I recognized why: It was *my* butt. *My* underwear. *My* rear—that great, white, wobbly bulb.

I was mortified. When did this happen? The visage was so foreign to me that I wouldn't have been able to identify myself from the back, even if my life depended on it. In fact, I could not remember the last time I'd fully looked at my backside—or my entire body, for that matter.

I had to keep reminding myself of the senior citizens from Michigan and true beauty and true balance in life and all the good stuff I'd just come to embrace as my actual reality. I was my own philosophical cheerleader, but my chants were a bit under-enthused.

It's hard work keeping the correct template in front of you as you navigate any given day. Attitude is everything. I reminded myself of this all the way home as I fought buyer's remorse. I kept visualizing the financial calculators and my paltry future and the money I'd just spent. It was all a chorus of doom until I glanced at the clock on my dash and realized that it was nearing sundown. I'd managed to keep my sunrise and sunset promise thus far, and I intended to keep it that day too.

I pulled off the beachfront road onto a small patch of hard dirt facing the sun. As I turned off the engine and stared, the chorus of self-flagellation quieted down. For a series of healing minutes, I lost myself in the magnificence of the template of creation. The sun shimmered with the color of late autumn maple leaves. Spontaneously, a verse from the Bible came to mind: "When I consider your heavens, the work of your fingers, the moon and the stars, which you have set in place, what is man that you are mindful of him, the son of man that you care for him?"[15]

My faith, like an underground ocean, runs beneath all my planning and dissecting. So burrowed into my vision and values, it exists almost imperceptibly between me and all I encounter. I relaxed into it.

I am as much a spiritual being as I am a physical being. And although I have not ignored that truth during this personal retreat, I have yet to deliberately plan for that area to grow and change. It's been so ingrained in me that I have almost overlooked it. I know that my faith is the cog of my existence, the center of my comfort. I walk about assuredly on its platform and sometimes take it for granted in the same way I take for granted that a floor will bear my weight. I don't consciously belabor the truth behind any of it, yet I utterly depend on the truth of all of it.

In the last moments of the sun's descent, I pictured myself diving headlong into it, flying like I do in dreams, effortlessly and with absolute peace. I envisioned a new page in my sketchpad with the heading "Spiritual." I imagined what I would write below it, but for the life of me, I couldn't picture what would come next. As the cold of dusk seeped into the car, I wondered if there was a plan that wouldn't look forced and arrogant under such a heading. I know enough to pray, and I do—as I have for all my life—but to write anything specific almost seems like putting limits on whatever is supposed to transpire in my life as directed by the One who created me. I don't and won't pretend to know all that His plan for my life holds. And I won't crawl into the box of how-tos in this area. I don't believe in using techniques to manipulate and direct God to act at my bidding, because, after all, if I could actually do that I would be God.

Making God act at my bidding. Not possible, and anyway I prefer "wrestling with the angels" for understanding and direction. I am sure the struggle for knowledge helps us discover for ourselves the living, relational side of God. It's not methodical—it's spontaneous.

Doing just that is a liberty I've been exercising as of late—trying to be more mindful of Christ as He directly reveals Himself to me. I want to know because I know through personal experience and direct relationship with Him. I want to be convinced because I am, not because someone told me to be.

Car lights now streak by me from either side. A lone tear escapes my eye for longings I don't know how to express. All I know is to pray, so I do. It is a simple prayer, with no bells and whistles:

> Give me eyes to see You, ears to hear You, and a heart to respond to all You reveal to me. Let the things that are impor-tant to You become important to me. Let all other things fall away in appropriate measure. Grant me grace when I stumble and veer too far off Your path. Give me mercy when I linger there too long. May this journey leave me more like You at the end than I was at the beginning.

And this prayer, perhaps, is what should guide the "Spiritual" page of my writings.

I am empty and full as I pull back onto the road, fittingly adjusted, momentarily untroubled by my idiosyncrasies and con-cerns, free in my smallness, in the humbling truth of my fragile life.

Chapter Fifteen

My Ultimate Epitaph

This afternoon I lie on the chaise lounge in my sweater. All this writing has raised a crop of small wool pills on my left sleeve. It looks like I fell into a patch of burrs.

About twenty feet overhead, a dart of herons flies away from the shore. I am in their flight route, and just like airplanes, their dramatic enormity is overwhelming when you're close enough to feel their wake.

I flip through my sketchpad, allowing the pages to brush against my thumb as they fall. I stop at "Relationships," where I am drawn to the names I'd noted. I realize I forgot an important segment in my recounting: people I need nothing from—the people I need to be there *for*, not the other way around. I wonder if most people would include this group of people in their lives, voluntarily, apart from the obvious family obligations.

The sun is about an hour away from going down. It holds no unusual hues, no rings of fire. It will be a very clean descent this evening. Last night's sunset and prayer stayed with me all throughout the day. I look down at the names on my list. Another door opens somewhere inside me.

To invest in others is important to me. This is as essential to my overall matrix as any other type of relationship. Nurturing, supporting, helping to grow someone gives me a sense of well-being, like I am depositing in the spiritual "bank of good"—that place where good deeds are recorded and we feel connected to one another in the ultimate expression of love, selflessness.

This realization rings a familiar bell, the one that intones dense with value. Fulfillment from dispensation. Gaining through loss. Riches through poverty. Sowing in hopes that somehow it will come back to me. In short, every bit of deity that can be expressed through flesh—perfect good flowing from imperfect people.

And as I consider this, I recognize that it agrees with all of me—not only with this moment in time, this year, this decade, but with all of me. Perhaps it's my true definition of a successful life, my life's endeavor, my ultimate epitaph:

Leaving behind all the bits of good that one can leave.

I purposefully slow my breathing as the last eighth of the sun falls earthward. Drawing in a long breath and exhaling softly, I admit that it is past time for me to own what my definition of success is, apart from what's been held up to me. In little areas like vacuuming and crumb control, I've had my ideas. And even in the obvious things like musical performance and annual income. But the overall template, the one on which most other areas are based—no, I hadn't adequately considered its measure, its scale.

It makes me tired to even consider the thought of tackling something so huge. Honestly, at this point in the evening, all I want is to consume some "cheat" food. Bean Burrito Supreme with hot sauce from Taco Bell. I roll off the chaise and tug at the back of my hair with my hand. I will, after all, need to be presentable for the drive-through lady.

My definition of success as it pertains to Taco Bell: "Don't eat the burrito before you get home."

Chapter Sixteen

Questioning "Success"

*H*ate it. *Hate it. Hate it.* All to the little military ditty "Left, left, left-right-left." The nagging naysayer chorus is strong this morning, with new objections to the "fat-shakedown." *Your body wasn't meant to do this. You're too old to run. You're gonna get shin splints. Your breasts are gonna sag.* I can barely stay with it the first five minutes. But I am determined because I know that if I make the first five, the naysayers quiet down and I can make thirty.

I am hoping that all these life changes I'm contemplating will go like that too. If I can get through the first "five," silencing all the reasons why I am bound to fail, maybe I will hit the "zone"—the place where it is still hard but doable.

Success. It's a word that has been presenting itself to me for years now, whose definition is associated with everything from toothpaste to heart transplants. It's almost as stretched thin as the word *love.*

I emptied all the trash in the house this morning, and it went through my mind, "*Success!*" like a magician would say, "Wallah!" I think I've been congratulating myself for years for a well-executed trash purge, maybe because it's one of the few tasks I can start and finish successfully in ten minutes and feel organized by the results, no loose ends, all buttoned down. What a farce. As soon as the cans are empty, I start filling them up again. It's never ending. The absurdity of the trash/success equation prompted me to make a list. I wanted to see how many other things made me "feel" successful.

I started with Webster's definition: "favorable or desired outcome." ("Favorable" being a subjective word. One person's idea of favorable would not be so favorable to everyone.)

What is success to me? According to my own template, my own definitions? I wrote anything and everything that came to mind, both the absurd and the meaningful.

> *I feel successful or I've felt a favorable result when:*
>   *I finish something well.*
>   *I change something for the better.*
>   *I do the honorable thing.*
>   *I help.*
>   *I execute something with excellence.*
>   *I bring comfort.*
>   *I bring encouragement.*
>   *I improve at something.*
>
> *Or more specifically:*
>   *I help someone get what they need.*
>   *I empty all the trash in my house.*
>   *I play a musical piece with passion and excellence.*
>   *I am part of a link in the chain of comfort to someone.*
>   *I communicate well, to the point of comfort.*
>   *I am self-sufficient.*

And then the old chicken-and-the-egg conundrum presented itself: *Do I feel successful when I operate in my gifts? Or do the things I've excelled at become my gifts because they bring pleasure and so I revisit them, use them, refine them—creating more skillful gifts? Is there a connection between feeling like I've achieved a "favorable result" and the "gifts" I use to easily achieve a "favorable result" in a given area?*

Which brings up another consideration, another template to draw from: *Where do I naturally excel? Where do I feel brilliant and gifted? In what areas or tasks do I feel effective and unimpeded—emotionally and otherwise? Do I begin my template for success there?*

And if these areas of gifting are inherent in each of us, would it also follow that they would hint themselves to us throughout our lives in one way or another, from the first moment of cognizance to the final breath?

I wondered as I wrote this on my pad in Deep Pacific Blue crayon:

> *For years now, I've felt successful when*
> *these things happen:*
> *these things are present:*

I stared at the words a long time and tried to remember the earliest times I felt "great" about something I did.

I think it was when I was eight. In fact, eight was a landmark age for me. I got a cowboy hat. I picked up a snake. And I had my first music lessons—on violin.

The cowboy hat changed my world. Every time I put it on, I became someone else—dangerous and mysterious. I'd tip the brim to one side like Jane from *Bonanza*, and my expression would go somber, my language succinct. "Yes, ma'am" and "no, sir" were the extent of my words. Cowboys don't talk much. They have secrets.

They're not afraid of snakes either. Snakes are just part of the territory. But I think they'd draw the line at patching them up the way I did after I wrestled one out of my cat's mouth. With fear and trembling, I put the tiniest Band-Aid around the puncture wound left by the cat's fang. I ran in to get my sister to stand witness to my bravery. When we came back out to the stoop, there was just one small proof that I ever had the snake encounter—the tiny Band-Aid stood upright on end forming a perfect "O." The snake had long since slithered away, and the cat would have nothing to do with me.

The only time I think the cat despised me more was when I would practice my violin. The scratchy tones I took great pains to create served as sonic wind shear, plastering my cat's ears flat to his head, pinning them back until they were stiff flaps of protection. His "selectively deaf" position was apparently not enough because almost immediately, out he would run from my presence, with that prissy gait that only cats can deliver—the one that makes you feel gauche and uncultured as if your offense is so reprehensible that they're about to gag.

It didn't stop me from practicing. I loved the way the violin felt in my hands. I loved the noises it made, even the sour ones. And I loved the way that other people responded to it when it was right.

On a great day, my mom would sit in the corner of the dining room, with me at my music stand performing my latest conquest. From "Lightly Row" to "Three Blind Mice," her head tilted to one side, eyes closed, a slight smile playing across her lips. And after every piece, there would be kind encouragement and descriptions of how the music made her *feel.*

Frankly, she could have been rolling her eyes up into her head and grinding her teeth in pain, but I never knew it. I only understood there was a power in music to take people to other places—to interrupt their activities and transport them elsewhere. And if you chose the right music and presented it in the right setting, it could make someone feel—even feel better. It was the beginning of my love affair with music.

Was it because I was good at it? My mom would say that sometimes I was. I know she made me believe I was. But more than the satisfaction of presenting a skilled expression, it was the responses that the music would elicit that excited me as well—at eight and every year since. The ability to bring something good to the inside of a person, without the normal checks and balances that are in place when you are attempting to reach someone in ways they expect. Music bypasses the protective grid and goes directly to the heart. It is the gentle intruder, the unexpected comforter.

What excites me still about it all is the gift of being a part of some eternal chain of kindness, encouragement, and comfort. It's like standing in a direct beam piercing out from some distant heaven. It just feels good—good and sometimes even great. Like the time I played "The Snake Dance" on my violin while wearing my cowboy hat—nirvana.

Chapter Seventeen

Reinvention

The sky is overcast, gun-metal gray. Ever since my run this morning, I can't get warm. I think a winter storm is coming. The beach is deserted, and it seems even the seagulls are taking cover.

My success list has me unnerved—not because I haven't enjoyed success but because I've been operating my life based on principles that have been invisibly shifting underneath me. I keep reminding myself that I love what I do. I love my career, the way my life plays out most days. In fact, I planned for this. This is what I wanted.

It's not that I don't want it anymore. I just think my "markers" have changed, the things that make me feel significant and in the flow of God's will for my life. I can't figure out if I am changing or if these themes have been here all the time, waiting to come into focus, alluding to themselves through the joy I feel when certain parts of my life line up with them.

Maybe this is a normal part of maturing, the taking stock and reinvention. Maybe this is all as it should be: God's timing for me to move in different ways. The general feel of disconnect that drew me here might be exactly on time in my life. That idea soothes me a little.

• • •

I've been doodling in geometrics for the past hour. Long, straight lines created by a ruler, crisscrossing into sharp-edged domains— a jigsaw puzzle. Some I colored, and some I filled with cartoons. My fingertips are stiffened from the cold. A chill has settled into the metal spiral of my sketchpad and found its way downward through my jeans to my skin. My jaw is aching. I think I've been scowling.

I just looked at my calendar from last year and counted how many hours I worked on average over the course of several weeks, not including travel. The average was ninety. *Ninety hours.* I couldn't account for them.

I wrote notes to myself in the most miniature font I could manage:

> *Scheduling is a linear art.*
> *There is a beginning and an end.*
> *On the purest of days, there should be a straight line of activity from end to end.*

Concerns. Strategy. Free-form thoughts all over the paper.

> *My schedule does not control me.*
> *I control it.*
> *A short focused day is more productive than a long unfocused one.*

And goals:

> *I must get a handle on my schedule.*
> *I have to learn how to say no to unprofitable things.*
> *Time is breath. Breath is life.*
> *I need more time for me on a daily basis.*

Work and life in general, I am learning, are quite inconvenient, but surely a middle ground can be reached. I really don't want to go back to scrambling around trying to "get it all done." I have to find some peace in this area. I have to make some hard choices. I hate choices because there is always a 50 percent chance I will make the wrong one.

In trying to make sense of the hours I've spent overworking through the years, I recognize one solid truth: The labor-intensive, high-pressure, pending things get my attention while the more meaningful, long-term, disciplined needs stand by, waiting their turn, sometimes indefinitely. My attention goes to the loudest demand.

I've had the realization since being away from the demands that time is like a wallet to me. When you first encounter it emptied, it looks like it has oodles of room, like you will never be able to fill it up. Within a week, it's bulging with receipts and clutter to the point that you are a nuisance at the grocery store. If there is room, it will be filled. If there is time, it will be filled. It doesn't matter if you are working on a career or a family or both; time will get crammed with activity if it is not protected in a disciplined way.

I realize I haven't been making thoughtful choices. I've been afraid to choose incorrectly, and in response I just started doing everything that was presented to me, without considering the value of each thing.

And why? Because I hate unfinished business. It's why I like to take out the trash. It's done. A task that has successfully ended. Purged from my to-do list.

And it has to do with other people's perceptions too. I've unconsciously accepted a premise: If someone wants me to do something, I should. That's it. The end. As if there is no choice. As if it is wrong for me to consider whether or not it is serving me or

God. And that reaction, too, is based in fear. I don't want anyone to think that I don't follow through. I want to be seen as reliable.

Reliable. Not very inspiring. I can see it now:

Here lies Margaret, who was reliable.

Reliable. Not vanguard, not gifted. Not self-directed. Perhaps not even God-directed.

. . .

Since I've been disciplining myself to get up so early, I've found out there is a way to live in the predawn hours without feeling like you have sandpaper in your eyelids: Go to bed early. I am sleeping more peacefully now. Actually going unconscious at 9:00 p.m. And the weird thing is that *I like it*—everything about it.

There seems to be a leisurely pace to the early morning hours that I haven't found in any other part of the day. The world sleeps, and I have clarity. Long stretches of uninterrupted time to watch the sunrise and consider my life and my God. It's reclaimed time for me because it is time I would have frittered away comatose, dreading the moment I'd have to wake up and start the race again, always feeling behind. Always a little off-kilter.

So I love these hours, and I find peace in them. I want to continue this routine when I return home. Focus early, work hard, and then the hardest thing: Shut down. Turn off the business phone. And do whatever it is that I will do to relax. And even that, at some point, will have to have its own heading on the pad: "Leisure Time." What is it to me—apart from distracting myself with the TV? I want to learn to relax productively, in a way that disengages me without merely wasting time. I want time to count, the way I feel like it does in these early mornings.

I've also made a goal of having at least five days off in the month. I will probably be sick to my stomach the first few times I choose to say no in order to fulfill this goal, but I need to try.

I can do it, and I should do it. It's Sabbath.

It is not unreasonable.

. . .

Like a life-sized jigsaw puzzle, these dream/story exercises have made a pattern, falling into place to form a picture—my picture—of what success is to me:

> To enable and encourage others with any tools that I can
> successfully use.

The many irregular pieces that make it up—the details—they are secondary. It doesn't matter if it is with music, or writing, or speaking—or even juggling, for that matter. I will use anything to create a platform and gain a voice. Any means by which I can deliver encouragement.

This is what excites me. This is where I feel like I operate in a frictionless environment. This is where I feel fulfilled and un-hampered, as though I am contentedly swimming along with the current in a stream of energy. It is my gift—but not in the sense that I have recognized that phrase in the past—as if what I have to offer is a gift for other people. No, more plainly, it is a gift to me—a private one given to me by God. A simple, figurative place or feel-ing that gives me pleasure. And when I utilize it, when I enter into it and enjoy it, somehow there is a pebble-in-a-pond effect. The rip-ples connect to a gift and flow outward, affecting those who are near enough to feel it.

It reminds me of the way art operates and the definition of the art I heard on National Public Radio in an interview with Sister Wendy, the art expositor. The interviewer asked Sister Wendy what her personal definition of art was. Her answer was loosely this: Art takes you out of yourself, lifts you up and pulls you into something higher for a time, and then places you back at last, changed.

And *art*, according to *Webster's Dictionary*, is "human creative skill or its application."

Human creative skill. Creativity. Isn't that when we connect with our most passionate selves, the part of us that is in a flow, an unhampered exchange with the Creator? Isn't that when we connect to our gifts? I am energized as I consider connecting with passion creatively and offering something that lifts people out of themselves into a stream of possibilities. I want to be a conduit between the mortal and the eternal.

I think of Melissa, my friend, the equestrian, mucking the stalls at 6:00 a.m. in the fall, blanket-like air thickened by the smell of hay and horses. I see her taut back dictating the methodical motion of a shovel sliding over ground. A cadence of task performed in stillness, the movement lithe and well honed, with the hues of day highlighting her face. Her moving in what she loves. Her emanating a beauty so stunning, like the orb of an earthbound angel. Digging, bending, hypnotically lost in the passion of the task, not because she had to but because she wanted to. In that earthy display, traces of her profession as a public relations agent, running parallel with the mucking, the organizing, the creation of frictionless environment, the uncovering of beauty in the common stuff of life. A beauty unsurpassed, there in the shadows of the barn: gift meeting passion. A gift that was meant for no one but herself, yet the force of it playing out, affecting all who are close enough to stand witness.

What a magnificent, raw way to experience the moments we are given in life, if we could manage it. Gift outward—moving in all the grace and feeling that breath can afford. To live like that, not every once in a while but as much as possible—by living with the gift at the center of all the planning, all the aspiring, all the living, both mundane and grand.

It is the way I will attempt to continue from here: Gift outward, flow outward. My overriding questions in life will be: *Does this allow me to maximize my natural giftings? Does this afford me the opportunity to move in them?* I know that these questions won't apply in every single area, but I do think they will help me create a template from which I can grade the expenditure of time according to what I feel I am to accomplish by God's prompting.

Years ago my pastor talked about one decision making all the others for you. He was referring to Christianity and how it meshes with morality and character, saying things like, "If you follow Christ, you don't have to ask yourself if you should fudge on your taxes. That is one decision you don't have to make. You can't because you are Christ's, and that is not His character. That is just one of a million others you don't even have to consider under the covering of Jesus."

I think that for the most part, this conviction about time usage will bring the same sort of clarity. In and of itself, I believe it creates a plumb line. Tasks, requests—when held beside it—will become easier to delineate, good from nominal, wasteful from directed.

Chapter Eighteen

Life Art

I am surprised at how little I need. When I first arrived here, I thought I'd miss the convenience of having all my "stuff" nearby. I barely packed anything from home, yet I haven't wished for one thing since I've been here. In fact, I like the clarity that comes with not having all my stuff around me.

In a way, I dread going back to my own house. It is filled with years of stuff. I want to live more like this: focused and unencumbered. When I get home, I have to begin that wretched process of weeding out—something I hate to do because, inevitably, whatever I just purged, I *need* within a few weeks. Old cassette tapes, just filled with important information I need to have. Old paint that I might need to use in some recycling project that I'll never finish. Old buttons from garments long gone. Socks with holes in them. Plastic pieces that belong to things I can't even recall. All of it is immensely important before I throw it out and then immediately after it's gone. It's bizarre but true. It's just my bad, self-fulfilling prophecy: You always think you need what you don't have.

· · ·

At around eight thirty last night, I put down my latest Mary Higgins Clark novel and entered into that presleep state in which I write brilliant songs that I scarcely remember in the morning, apart from things like "reggie" rhyming with "veggie." I was dreaming about life art and how much I've missed experiencing it.

Like my mother and her African violets. I saw myself, barely tall enough to peer into the wooden bunks that housed the fussy flowers in our basement. I clearly recalled as if it were last week the habitual scene playing out morning and afternoon for years before I entered the first grade: our basement, smelling of potting soil, lit only by florescent plant lights; my mother, tending to what seemed like hundreds of purple African violets, row after row of furry leaf and perfect bloom, each a friend to her, each a project in need of nurturing and tenderness.

Sprigs of plastic marked each pot. Popsicle-size stakes, with names like "Clarissa" and "Sophie" written on them, in her unique cursive that slanted left, as if it were in a perpetual effort to halt. The beauty of her small hands sliding underneath certain leaves, gently lifting them to another angle for clarity. The soft tones she emitted when inspecting the blooms and the quiet precision with which she moved while alternately watering or pruning. Her answers to my many interruptions and her introductions of the various champions—as if they were old family friends—many winning her gold ribbons year after year.

To see her there in my mind is to see art come to life. Hand touching leaf. Eye scrutinizing form and shape. Fingers pruning imperfections that would never heal or serve. Reverence telegraphed by every sound, every movement she made.

These inclinations expressed themselves from plants to people, where my mother embraced and defended the broken and misshapen, as she demonstrated with a neighbor who struggled with an extreme case of bipolar disorder. For a time, he was mandated to an extended stay at a mental health facility for treatment. It was halfway through that stay when the shadow of his tall muscular frame stood at our front screen door. Without concern, my mother invited him in for a cup of tea, and he calmed down in the aura of her comforting demeanor. They shared a cup and were on their second when the phone rang, the police on the other end. She made no effort to hide the conversation and became indignant when they warned her that he was dangerous. Her response was simple and gracious: "Yes, he's here, and I am fine. We are having a cup of tea together. He's my friend. I am not worried."

My mom, connecting to the nurturer in her soul, moving in her gift, forming beauty, her gift soothing the agitated and finding the beauty in brokenness. It was life art, I am sure, directed and implanted by God.

I played these images over and over in my head until I drifted off. My last thoughts were of DNA and how I hope that along with the tangible connections, the spiritual predispositions are dispensed similarly.

• • •

I am at the dining room table, looking out at two men surfing, or attempting to. The only time this section of the Gulf is even close to surfable is after a storm; otherwise, the waves act more like bay waves. Today they are kicking up and the tide is out, so all of it works together for a nice ride.

The men are in wet suits. Judging by their technique, they infrequently have the opportunity to surf. They've been at it for hours now and show no signs of staying on their boards for more than twenty seconds.

In front of me on the table is a fresh page. On it I have written two words: "Mission Statement." I've decided to incorporate a little business acumen into the overall style of arranging my life, my art. I am attempting to come up with an overall mission statement for my life. A succinct one-to-two-line description of what I deem to be the overarching principle for my life. What my ultimate goal is for all my years here on earth. The big goal. It's so obvious. I don't know why I didn't think to do it a long time ago.

In my business, a mission statement gave me a clear definition of purpose and streamlined all the various decisions that arose concerning day-to-day details. Here in my personal mission statement I will apply the same criteria. It will transcend age and career tools and apply to personal life as well as public life—kind of like an overall theme for my existence. I'll take what I've already determined about me, what success means to me, and insert it into a statement that will be a marker. Once it is set, I'm sure it will help me gauge all my planning and dreaming. It probably won't fit perfectly, but I know it will at least help bring me more clarity. On my paper, I finally arrive at:

To uplift and encourage people.

I ask myself if that is enough for a whole lifetime.

To uplift and encourage people.

Is that statement big enough? Is that really the sum total of what I want to do on planet earth, aside from all the specifics, aside from all the tools?

I mull these questions over as I unconsciously run my thumb over one lone coarse hair growing from the bottom of my chin. I can't believe this is happening to me—the chin hair, that is.

My Aunt Agnes had four like this, and they always fascinated me. The fact that she never plucked them seemed like a flip-off to the world, as if she was daring anyone to mention them.

I wonder if there is some kind of medical explanation for this. Like you hit thirty, and a coded message expresses itself in your DNA: "Begin coarse facial hair extension, zone 2." Is there no end to the surprises of aging?

I can't concentrate until I pluck it, so I go inside and do the deed, careful not to scrutinize everything else that could possibly be going on from the neck up. It's funny how a tiny hair can make me feel so bad at first and, once plucked, that much better. It's my obsession with small annoyances and small relief. I think I carry it throughout the rest of my life as well. I focus on the tiny things— things I shouldn't be concerned with at all.

As I lean back in the sun and lift my new unoccupied hair shaft to the sunlight, I wonder, *How far down the ladder from my mission statement does one lone facial hair fall?* I don't care. I couldn't rest until it was removed.

I consider the anarchist in me who wants to be reckless and carry on Aunt Agnes' hair legacy: No plucking. I think about it hard for about a minute. Who am I kidding? I am not that brave—not yet anyway.

Back to the mission statement. If I were a corporation trying to move goods and justify my existence, would this mission statement be enough to build on? Yes. To help people to feel better about themselves and find the resources they need in order to move forward and grow—yes, that would be some product. This statement is built on my giftings, and it is broad enough to encompass the smallest of moves. It is large enough to build an industry on.

I'm satisfied with that, as far as I can understand it right now anyway. I watch two joggers passing by at the water's edge. Along with them comes a cold breeze that prickles the left side of my head—a sure sign that I am pillow-bald there. I haven't combed my hair since last night. That, too, is an improvement.

• • •

Tonight I have Lena Horne on the stereo. Her voice is comforting in a nostalgic way. It is the voice of the forties and fifties, when men wore top hats and overcoats and women leaned into their lover's arms as they strolled. It reminds me of a picture of my parents walking down a Manhattan street together in the same era. They look like movie stars.

Lena's voice is like a mother's voice: resonant, but mature, unapologetic vibrato. I think it is what my own mother's voice would've sounded like if she weren't tone deaf, which she was determined to be in Catholic school, where the chief request of the nuns was that in music class she would only "mouth" the words.

I never knew it though. I can remember endless days of singing with her—in the car, tending the violets. Always folk songs of some sort, like "I See the Moon." It all sounded great to me. It wasn't until my own introduction to music in elementary school, and my subsequent visit to the nurse's office for a hearing test, that I discovered that sometimes the notes go up and down and that not every song is a dirge.

I'm dreaming again now, reviewing my life stories and casting my net wide. The more I examine my mission statement, the more I realize it's about communication, and communication is all language. So my tools must be words—written, spoken, sung—in more languages than just my own.

This forms my personal vision statement—the way that I will accomplish my mission statement:

Through communication, books, music, speaking—encourage and uplift people.

This is certainly broad enough to last my lifetime, and I already know I will want to accomplish this forever because it is based on the part of me that has not changed—the part of me that comes to life when engaged.

Chapter Nineteen

The Shoe Incidents

I was entering the interstate this morning, on my way to Pensacola, when I noticed a lone sneaker on the shoulder of the on ramp. Someone's sneaker. Someone's shoe.

They're so personal—shoes. They are necessary items, bearing the brunt of life as they transport us to and fro, and on them the stuff of life clings in dust, dirt, watermarks. Shoes are one of the few things that go with us everywhere and illustrate the wear and tear we experience every day. They tell the story.

As I sped by the sneaker, I wondered, *How did it get here? And where is the other one?*

When I was little, I had my own shoe incident. At three, I had red, hard leather orthopedic shoes. I remember one thing about them: I hated life when they were on my feet. They laced up to my ankles, pinching my limbs the whole way. It wasn't because they weren't properly sized either, because I recall an exasperated trip back to Thom McCann for a consultation. They were the right size, all right, and expensive too. But they just weren't the right shoes for me. They functioned, but they hurt.

The "shoe incident" folklore went like this:

Apparently, upon returning home one afternoon from a grocery run, my mother noticed I was wearing only one shoe. After the familiar scolding about taking care of my shoes and not taking them off, she searched the car. No sign of the shoe. No amount of interrogation yielded any results. I just plain did not know what happened to the shoe.

When my father arrived home from work, there were hushed exchanges and skeptical expressions. He had his try with me, but still no answer.

Two days later, our next-door neighbor knocked on the door. "Peg, thought you might be looking for this," she announced. In her hand was the other shoe.

"Oh my gosh, Dorothy! Was it in your yard?" my mother gasped.

"Well, you're not gonna believe this," she answered. "I was down at the diner on Main Street, and as I got out of my car, I saw it laying in the parking lot. I knew immediately it was Margaret's shoe."

"The Woodland Diner?" my mother asked in disbelief. It's over a mile away from our house. We passed it every time we drove. I loved that diner. Root beer floats.

My mother turned to me, questions scurrying across her eyes. "Margaret, did you throw your shoe out the car window?"

I shook my head no. I had no memory of it. I was sure of that.

There is that moment when parents decide whether or not they should press a matter. I saw my mom decide against it. Dorothy and my mom went into the other room for coffee. They took the shoe with them.

I have since pictured my chubby little hand working the shoe off my foot in the backseat of the Buick. Holding on to the heel, watching the scenery pass until the right moment, then a simple lob out the window, toward the diner.

I probably didn't remember because I didn't feel guilty. A part of me knew the shoe wasn't good for me, and that part of me did the only sane thing: got rid of it. It was a relief not to have to wear those shoes anymore. And while the lone shoe was missing, my mom had bought another pair. They felt much better.

It's how I feel right now, driving toward downtown. It's like I've thrown a faulty shoe out the window all over again. The lone shoe that bore my weight. The object that transported me from here to there—my underlying support system. I've replaced it with something that feels better to me, although some would probably argue the point.

It feels good to be free.

Chapter Twenty

Renewal

I bought *Muscle and Fitness* today. It took some guts to lay it on the counter at Kroger alongside my sunblock. I hope the clerk knew I was buying it for health reasons and not to gawk at the guys in their "show suits." How embarrassing.

It was the only magazine of its kind that had in-depth information about nutrition and working out written in a way I could understand. Still, the cover was over the top. A massive man in a tiny Euro bathing suit, glistening under the lights.

Truth be known, I ultimately did buy it for the pictures—one picture, in fact, of a seventy-five-year-old man. His body, his skin, his abs were beyond reality. He looked amazing. It was as if he had defied time. His advice? Keep lifting weights, and watch what you eat.

They always make it sound so easy. I've done crunches until I want to curse, and the closest I've ever come to a six-pack is something like a three-pack of hot dog buns. I'd settle for a tight one-pack if I could get it.

Aim high. It's what I kept thinking when I looked at my AARP hero in his show shorts.

• • •

My time here is racing by now. Last night at dusk, I came out onto the deck to watch the sun go down. It was freezing cold, brittle, like ice was in the air. I kept shifting back and forth from foot to foot in order to stay warm. There was none of the spectacular color display that I've witnessed for weeks now, just a clean red-orange ball slowly slipping down the horizon.

I swept the vista from right to left, hoping to record it in my mind's eye forever, like a living video. When I reached the end of my own semicircle, I noticed the moon was already fairly high in the sky behind me.

It seemed strange; the moon and the sun sharing the same sky at dusk. I couldn't ever remember it happening before. Back and forth between the two visages I went, considering how many things seemed strange to me now. Maybe I had seen this scene in particular some time in the past, but if I had, I never noted it—like so many other things, apparently.

I have loved these quiet days. I have gulped them like air, worn them through like the soles of shoes. They have indeed transported me from one dimension to another and deposited me here—with fresh vision, new life, renewed sense of "being."

Yet for all their tranquility and decadent ease, they have not ensnared me. I know they are for only a time. Only effective for this season, this purpose—now. To elongate or worship them would be wrong. To desire them as supreme and superior would be foolish. They are a means. They are tools. I cannot hoard them. They are sustenance for now, meaningful in this moment, corruptible when out of context, meant to get me to the next level of life.

So with my lists and edicts, I begin to pack. With my hopes and resolutions, I precariously move forward, accountable to only myself and my wildest dreams.

If I fail, only I will know. If I succeed—well, I might tell a few people.

Part Three

Breathing Free

The best things in life are nearest: Breath in your nostrils,
light in your eyes, flowers at your feet, duties at your hand,
the path of right just before you. Then do not grasp at the stars,
but do life's plain, common work as it comes, certain that
daily duties and daily bread are the sweetest things in life.
—ROBERT LOUIS STEVENSON

Chapter Twenty-One

Braving the Elements

"Where does this go?"

It's the UPS man, holding the first of several large packages that contain the new dining room chairs I'd ordered from a favorite catalog.

"Right here in the living room." I wave him in, sure of its final destination. It's so unlike the last time I had to answer that question three months ago—from the moving van. Then I hardly heard the inquiry over Max's barking. Turning from the ten-dollar piano that awkwardly blocked the doorway to the kitchen, I replied to Percy, one of the movers, "Downstairs, in the basement." He and his two helpers stood in the living room, sweating profusely. On the floor in front of them was my weight bench. Percy wiped his forehead with a white handkerchief limp from moisture.

"Margaret, lemme ask you somethin': Doesn't *anything* go here on the main floor?" With that, Percy and his coworkers chuckled and plopped down on the bench. I know I must have been their worst nightmare. Treadmill, dumbbells from three to thirty-five pounds, weights, boxes of CDs and books not yet sold, seven years' worth of filed records. I still didn't know where everything would go yet. I'd never lived in a house like this. A "Grand Old Lady," my mom would call it, early 1900s, replete with ten-foot ceilings, wood floors, and the requisite lack of closet space. I just happened to see it while killing a lazy February afternoon visiting open houses. Like so many other changes over the past decade, words and formulas escape me when I try to explain what made me go from looker to doer. I saw this house and I knew I would be happy here.

More than a decade has passed since I packed up from my beach retreat and came back to Nashville. I never planned to move from my hillside retreat just west of the city, at least not seriously. Over the years, I'd developed a Sunday-morning ritual that centered on the real estate section of the paper, but I never was seriously "looking." It was more like a flirtation with the concept of "space," new space, cleared space. I don't understand it, really. Maybe it's the mystery of potential—the lives, the relationships and tasks that could be lived out in a space. Or maybe it has just represented change, forward movement, chances not yet taken.

Chances. Change. A 180-degree turn, in my case. I have made that costly journey from fear to pursuit when it comes to change. Eleven years ago, unrest was staring me in the face. My life disconnect led me to a plan, a plan for change. It scared me, the idea of letting go of the familiar for the unknown. But I was ready. And "ready," as a believer in divine direction, is sometimes so uncontrollable. There is a timing that exists in another dimension. It makes you ready, or uncomfortable, or brave. It gives you wings, or stops you dead in your tracks.

My thoughts and feelings about the kinds of change that resulted from braving the elements—external and internal—during my beach retreat have morphed from alien to comfortable, terrifying to joyful. The marriage of *significance* and *fulfillment* that now blesses my soul is the sweet reward that comes only after an initial leap of faith. The many pockets of peace that have settled into my interior are the result of risk and commitment. Wouldn't it be nice if the prize was there before the leap, grandly rolled out like a red carpet, inviting all into its chamber? I would appreciate that kind of clarity, but I have found it only in hindsight.

For a long time in my life, I felt significant and fulfilled, but then those essential states of being began to seem fragile and airy, like ethereal cloud formations overhead. They were no longer solid ground beneath my feet. The reunion of fulfillment and significance has been rich and meaningful, but I can't pretend to know exactly what factors procure it. I do know that people I never expected to find it have, and those who seem to most deserve it miss it. Untidy, this experiential truth. God seems to like to confound our pea brains. But I have made peace with this—and that too is change for me.

● ● ●

The UPS man makes me sign for the chairs, and he is on his way. Max, my four-year-old golden retriever, has made fast friends with him after giving his shoes a good sniff. Somehow this guy registered "okay." It's an inexact science I will never comprehend.

I ignore the chairs because there are bigger fish to fry. Moving—as a full-fledged adult—is a massive task. Though I've been here twelve weeks, I am still unpacking. "A little each day" has been my motto since the first night I slept here. It's the only way I know to do this without getting lost in the basement black hole.

There are plenty of boxes I still haven't opened. Obviously, I must not need what's inside them. In an act of newfound spontaneity, I threw out one loosely labeled "Garage" and another labeled "Bathroom—important." I've used all of my tools and toilet paper since I've been here, so anything in either of those boxes would probably hold the value equivalent to a crimping iron, Aquanet, and half-used containers of Spackle.

I feel differently about the boxes in "my" room though. The roofline of the cozy rectangle add-on upstairs is dormered, giving it the feel of a cozy chapel. The walls and the carpet are a calming cream, serene and soft on the senses. At one end of the short rectangle, the sun rises; at the other it sets. It's a perfect place to observe the display that takes place at the beginning and end of each day.

Before I tackle the boxes, I take a glance out the window at my tiny "Eden." I watch as Max busies himself chasing the neighbor's cat in the backyard. I know these special boxes hold the stuff of life, both joyful and sad. I'm ready to categorize, separate, and tag them as best I can, if memories can stand such analysis and captivity.

A cool glass of water in hand, I plop down on the floor, cross-legged in the middle of mayhem. Deep breaths. Silence. Reflection. I take my time as I envision how all my favorite things will lay out along the walls. All the photos, trinkets, writings, and keepsakes that have made the "cut" are now standing up for their just due. Along with all the pictures and mementos, I will put out my books that run the gamut of Indians to architecture. And my toys too. My erector set. My punching nun. A reclaimed cigar box my sister filled with sand and shells for me after one visit to the beach. I've excused myself from keeping the room neat, because I am the only one it will serve. It's the perfect place to be a mess, a perfect place to be embarrassed. A perfect place to note, respect, and grieve change and to store and display all that is dear and quirky to me.

Along one wall, in a soft fold, lay a group of papers I've already unpacked. They are the written account of various beach pilgrimages, park escapes, and mountain retreats dating back to the Howard. What began then as a one-time desperate attempt to gain some perspective has since become an annual ritual. For a long time, the Howard was my desired haven, kicking off with a shared weekend with friends over New Year's. The gathering together of some of my favorite people started spontaneously. While honoring my conviction about becoming more responsible with relationships, I'd put out the call to "my people." In a ragged flow, they'd fly, drive, and drag themselves into my peaceful world for late-night rummy games and morning beachcombing.

The high point of the week was always the midnight picnic on the beach, where we'd share our new resolutions and the various jewels we'd gleaned from the past year's difficulties. Those nights left us both humored and humbled as we huddled against the wind and placed it all in the hands of God. Seated in a circle, praying for one another, thanking Christ for all of it—both understandable and mysterious—became a visible commemoration of what I'd wished for: the gathering of God's chosen family in my sphere.

My annual Sabbath started after the new year began and the last person left. There, alone with nothing to distract me, I'd carefully lay out the prior year's pages along with the very first set I made. I'd compare and marvel. Not a year went by in which I didn't accomplish at least 85 percent of what I'd set out to do—things I'd never have known I wanted to do or should do had I not written them down.

This winter retreat became something I fiercely protected. The Howard became the first of many different places I escaped to. Eventually, my little secret haven became the favorite of far wealthier people, and I had to search for the next beach "view," the next pocket of peace.

Some of these Sabbaths brought more rest than radical change. Once the groundwork had been laid on the first trip, it was a matter of following through. In some areas, that meant a few aggressive actions early on, with a few "maintenance" ones along the way. Those years, where the work was set in motion and there was little to adjust, were confusing at first. Used to being in motion, I'd second-guess everything, sure that I was a slug or just plain deceived. But with maturity came self-acceptance and confidence.

Now when a retreat brings mostly play, I indulge, without a pang of conscience or fear.

In my cocoon-like room, I take up the original papers from the Howard. The outermost offerings are leaves from the first big sketchpad I bought on my foray to the Super K so many years ago. Marked with crayons and watercolors, scribbled with goals and per-mission not to have goals, the loose folio might as well have been my first writing tablet or my first pair of running shoes. They embodied the "first" in a series of dreams, visions, and actions that altered the course of my life; they were a physical marker of my catharsis. Tanned from the years, the leaves stand experienced like firstborns in this colony of meaning. Their DNA runs throughout most every picture, every journal, every memento, stretching back to before they were ever created, because without them, none of this would have come to be.

Although I know the leaves by heart, I pull them into the bright light for a fresh look. Looking at them is like leaning over a precipice—a ledge in my life where I can review with clear perspec-tive the experience and wisdom I have gained since I aired out, dreamed wide, and came to.

At the top of my first page is a picture of my inspiration lady. She is one of the figures I cut out of a magazine on that initial retreat. I used the scissors and Elmer's glue I bought to create beings and visions that entertain only me. Pasted into those first pages of the art pad: a big clock with the universal circle-slash that com-municates NO; single letters in various fonts, comprised like a ran-som note, forming phrases like, "Life peace," "You must," and George Anderson's mantra, "Life flies by. Enjoy it." I cut out things that were lovely to look at, like a blue Belize sea and a face poised in a peaceful expression. Of course, there were the other ensembles, like a gargantuan high-heeled shoe floating in the middle of the ocean, bug legs on a lady's body, a fat baby head and diaper on a bodybuilder. "Curious decoupage," I call it. As with the coloring, my multimedia art instincts served as yet another way for me to connect all my senses with a concept. While cutting with my hands, imaging with my mind, considering with my heart, and breathing in that familiar grade-school Elmer's scent, my "grown-up buttoned-down self" jarred into a freer place.

The inspiration lady was my aspiration model. It is a simple black-and-white photograph of an elderly woman caught in mid-twirl of a fox trot embrace with a handsome elderly man. Her face is deeply lined, beautiful with history. Her head is thrown backward in delight as she clings to her partner. They are the picture of Western vitality. I am aspiring to be this woman: lively, unafraid, celebratory, taking in every last drop life has to offer with reckless abandon.

I will be earthy and a bit eccentric, but I will be wise. I wrote that aspiration in my very first "Wildest Dreams" life story, projecting ten years ahead. Now, eleven years later, I am on target—even down to the "bit" part. I'm officially on only the second "c" of "eccentric." My mom made it all the way to the last one. I'm taking my time. I still need something to aspire to.

· · ·

My sister, on the other hand, is on the "n"—something I confirmed when she moved into her new apartment. She needed company and someone who could do the Home Depot runs. I volunteered and flew to Long Island for a few days. On the drive to her place from the airport, she began her warnings.

"Now, don't get too excited," Kate cautioned. "It's not that nice. In fact, there are a few things that are not great." She guided the Toyota SUV down the tiny main street that paralleled the South Shore of Long Island.

"I'm sure it's fine," I said, waving my hand to dismiss her concerns.

"Well, there *is* the Long Island Railroad," she countered, tipping her head to one side.

"What about it?"

Kate explained. "The East Line sort of runs through my backyard."

"What? The train runs through your backyard? You can't be serious!" I exclaimed.

"It's not *that* bad."

"How far from the house?"

"Um, I'd say about sixty feet."

"The train runs through your backyard, about sixty feet from your house," I said, matter of fact, making sure I understood her right.

"Yes," she answered, "and then there's the highway."

"The highway."

Kate continued, "The highway runs in front of the house, where my bedroom is."

I considered this. "Okay," I replied, letting a deep breath out, both palms facing forward. "The highway runs at the front door and the train at the back door."

"That's most of it."

"How do you get any sleep?" I asked as I faced her, just to see if this is a practical joke. I waited for her to crack a smile. She focused straight ahead.

"I'm getting used to it. It's bad only when the windows are open," she answered. "There's no air conditioning."

No air conditioning? It didn't make sense. Of all the apartments that were out here, this *was the only one she could find?* I didn't know what to say. We sat in silence at a red light.

"Can you actually *see* the people on the train as they go by?" I asked.

"Yeah. At night, sometimes I see them looking back at me too. I wave."

"You *wave?*

"Sometimes," she answered.

"Are you in your backyard when you're doing this?"

"Not exactly."

"Where then?"

She giggled under her breath. A secret was about to come out. "In my bathroom," she replied.

"In your—*ugh!* Do you think that's wise? There are a lot of crazy people out there. Wouldn't be too hard to find you . . ."

"I know, I know. I'm careful," she assured me.

Exasperated, I stopped the inquisition. *How on earth can you be careful when you are standing in your own bathroom waving to strange commuters in your backyard?*

We pulled up in front of the apartment, which sure enough was fronted by the highway and backed by the railroad tracks. "This is it!" Kate said excitedly.

I grabbed my suitcase out of the back of the SUV and made my way to the back door. I heard a train whistle in the distance. It was dusk. The ground began to rumble beneath our feet, and within seconds the double-decker train went whizzing by, blurry with people reading the paper or aimlessly looking out the window, all silhouetted by the soft yellow glow of the cabin lights. We both stopped to look.

When the noise subsided, I admitted, "It's kind of pretty in a mechanistic urban way."

"I know what you mean!"

As we walked into the kitchen, I started to feel her excitement.

I felt so comforted in her presence. I wondered why we had waited so long to get together again. She had her relationship and I had my career, both very all-consuming for too long a time. Her relationship had ended and I'd "come to." Standing in her neat, small space, I wondered if she was considering the same things I was—like time and how short it is, how deliberate you must be about sharing it with others.

A quick glance around told me that the kitchen was the largest room, a far cry from the cottage she has lived in for the past seven years.

"And here is the living room. It's kind of small, but I like it," she said.

It was miniscule, but if anyone knew how to live in tight spaces, it was Kate. You don't live in New York your whole life without learning that.

"I want to paint it," she added.

"What color?"

"Well, funny thing is that when I signed the lease, I asked the landlord if I could paint in here. I think I surprised him, because most people are here and gone within six months," she explained.

"What'd he say?"

"Sure—just don't paint it any weird color like yellow."

"What color do you want to paint it then?" I asked.

"Yellow," she said succinctly.

We both laughed out loud. I knew right then and there that I would be the voice of rebellion that weekend and get her to paint it yellow.

"Well, let's do it, then," I said. "It's small enough to finish in a day."

Kate looked surprised. "Why Margaret, I thought you were the law-abiding citizen of the family!"

I shook my head, minimizing the landlord's request. "I think he meant like 'baby's room yellow' or 'overly happy yellow.' We'll find a Pottery Barn yellow. He won't even think it's yellow," I explained.

"But what if he doesn't like it?" she asked, speaking from the cautious DNA in both of us. Kate didn't know I'd been genetically altered since she'd seen me last.

"Does *he* live here—in *this* room?" I asked with a half smile, gesturing toward the lone window.

"No." She nervously giggled.

"And aren't you the model tenant in all the other ways that one can be? Waving to the train, keeping everything clean, playing your music at a reasonable volume, not cooking with too much garlic?"

"Yeah, I guess I am," she answered, surveying the room and mentally calculating the time needed to complete the task.

"Then let's do it, Kate. It's *your* living room—you're paying for it. *You* have to sit in it night after night. *You* have to live here, not him. You need something soothing and cheery, something to signal the start of your new, nonconformist life. We are painting this place yellow—tomorrow," I announced, sealing the statement with my most convincing nod.

"But wait, I'm not sure," she said, pulling at her eyebrow with her thumb and forefinger, a habit she's had since we were kids.

"Kate, what's the big deal? If he says to change it back, I'll hop a Southwest flight and come to change it back. It will take us only a few hours," I reasoned.

"Okay, we'll do it!" she agreed and then turned to me. "Boy, Margaret, when did you become so brave?"

Classic George Anderson tumbled out before I could even think about it: "Life flies by. Enjoy it."

Chapter Twenty-Two

Testaments

I've been sitting in my special room, knees tucked under me, for what feels like hours. Pins and needles are surely not far behind. To my left is a pile of pictures bound for my trash can. It's massive. What was I thinking when I tried to take a picture of giraffes on safari in Kenya? I can't even tell what's in that picture. It just looks like windblown fruit trees. And how many pictures of sunrises and sunsets does one truly need? They are all spectacular, but instead of reminding me of the incredible moments when I experienced them, they just look like nice postcards.

Makes me wonder if I should spend less time trying to document special moments in God's presence with hard-edged obtrusions like cameras and use the time instead to fully enjoy them. Perhaps some things were never meant to be one-dimensional. Almost every photo that contained landscape or scenery looked flat, especially Africa. Nothing could capture its beauty other than the faces of the people. I kept the pictures of those, both the joyful and the tragic.

Almost fifteen years have passed since I first heard about a humanitarian organization that intervenes in poor areas, helping the people find solutions to their ongoing difficulties. I knew right away that their work was something that resonated with me. World Vision didn't know of me, but I was determined to get on their map. For a few years I even followed their primary public representative around at various functions, trying to preach all the great reasons I should present their charity to my supporters. Up until that time, they didn't have many spokespeople presenting World Vision's cause to a music audience. I knew that their mission of finding sponsors, people who send a monthly financial gift to a child that not only benefits the child but helps the whole community as well, would strike a chord with people who valued my work. My own heart was pierced the first time I laid eyes on one of World Vision's simple folders that contain the picture of one child along with his or her abridged life story. The needs were simple too: fresh water, food, basic medicine, and education. Since encountering World Vision's solution, I knew I would never cease to be haunted by how little it takes to save another human being from devastation. Thirty-five dollars every thirty days.

I've sponsored or "adopted" children through this program for years now. I frame their pictures and treasure their letters. My journey with World Vision and children all over the world has come a long way from my early futile encounters with that representative, whose attention I couldn't seem to get no matter what I did. In fact, time after time, he fled me, once even up to his hotel room, where his feeble offering before the door clicked securely shut was, "Yeah, um, I'll call you." I stood in front of the solid cherry door and spoke to it since he was officially gone. "I don't think you have my number." He didn't open the door.

Later that day, I sat at dinner with friends and explained my dilemma. Lucy spoke up first.

"Well, Margaret, is he single?"

"Yeah, but I don't know what that's got to do with it."

"Is he cute?" she continued.

"Yeah, but why is that an issue?" I sputtered back.

"Margaret," she leaned in closely with a serious look on her face, "maybe he thinks you want his body."

Before I could reason it all out, I blurted, "Lucy, I don't want his body. I just want his children!"

Heads throughout the restaurant snapped around, and I felt the cherry-red flush on my face.

But indeed, that was all I wanted. I knew that World Vision's objective was to support needy children and their families all over the earth, to love them tangibly, to change their futures for the better—and all because Christ commanded us to love. I wanted to be involved.

When the cranky, cute single guy finally moved on to bigger and better things, one of the first encounters I had with the World Vision ministry took place in Africa. It was their belief that if I was asking to be involved, and if I was to represent their work to anyone, I needed to experience it in its entirety.

That first visit to Kenya was life altering. I don't think there are words with enough edge, enough precision and pathos, to express the full impact of standing in the middle of Third World poverty as a westerner. Babies with babies perched on their hips, children emaciated from the effects of AIDS. Little ones squatting on heaps of garbage, slowly working through debris, looking for anything to eat or trade for food. The smells of humanity in all its raw forms. And hardest of all, the eyes—empty and without any reason to hope, reason to live, reason to be.

After that trip, I began to present World Vision's cause to audiences around the world. I have found that not only did I want to be involved in using every tool I had to impact poverty and sickness but that it gives me great satisfaction to be a link in the chain of comfort to someone. World Vision and their mission aligned deeply with my own—with my core values and specific goals I had recorded on my first beach retreat. The first of several outlets for my dreams of being "provision" to others, I found a natural alignment between my propensities and God's plan to meet a need, and in it was an even greater blessing: God's answer to my prayer for children. I wanted children. I'd stopped asking by the time I finally saw the gem of His provision.

That happened shortly after I received a new box of fresh faces who had not found a sponsor. As per my own tradition, I put the box on a table in my foyer where I could see it, so I would be reminded to pray for those kids, to pray someone chooses to support them when I spend a little time at each event I participate in, talking about their plight. The eyes of my soul were opened wide one day as I walked by the photographs and said one of my usual prayers: "Lord, please help Your children find homes in the hearts of people who can help them." There was no fanfare, just an audible echo: "*Your* children."

I stopped dead in my tracks. I stared at the photo of the little boy on top, in his bright blue wrap. God's children. *My* children. My heart breaks for them. My soul grieves for them. I can hardly look at their individual photos without breaking down or robbing a bank to save them. *My* children.

Yes, God gave me my children. Definitely not in the way I expected Him to—not even close—but by a more dynamic means, one that serves many. And seeing this miracle with new eyes, I felt a fat dose of God's provision giving me "fullness of joy." I wonder if it is similar to the blessed relief those kids feel when they get the news that someone has adopted them through World Vision's program— that someone in the world truly cares about them and will take care of them.

• • •

I am keeping things that remind me of God's intricate, mysterious provision. They are most often the common things: a piece of drift-wood gleaned from the bottom of a lake, my father's pocketknife, a picture of me drawn by a four-year-old from Baltimore. I don't know how to arrange them all. It's the same problem I'm having with the photos. How do I group them? By content? By decades?

As with my photographs of the African children, men, and women, the faces of the friends before me are most engaging. How young we all were at some point, and how unknown to each other. But as friendships survived and adjusted, how easy it is to look back now and see the hidden emotions in the early years. Something as simple as a smile takes on deeper meaning when you *really* know someone.

I've pulled a picture out of the pile to frame. It's of some of those people who have become part of God's provision for my life, the friends who have stuck around and have seen me through the worst and best. The need to be known: It is clear in this shot of our New Year's beach group. We must have asked a passerby to take it, because we are all sitting cross-legged in the sand, leaning against one another in a crash of laughter. No makeup, a sandcastle in front of us. Only Joyce is really paying attention to the task, squinting against the sun toward the lens. But even she laughs, because I'm sure she knows that no one will sit pretty for the camera in an orderly fashion. It's just the way it is when we all get together. These relationships worked for some quirky, hard-to-explain reason. They aren't laborious—not most of the time, anyway. The chemistry is difficult to describe. It's just that we seem better all together than apart, the sum of us greater than any one.

That year, in usual tradition since our first retreat together, I got to our location a little early to prepare the house. One of my great-est pleasures is to find the most comfortable setting for all of us to enjoy one another *and* to stock it with everyone's favorite things. The Howard was booked, so this Mediterranean beachfront villa was the next best thing. Inside its three stories were enough bedrooms for each of us to spread out, and we would surely spend relaxing hours taking in God's creation from the rooftop terrace.

It was late in the evening, and I had just finished lighting candles around the house, when they tumbled in, exhausted from the long road trip from the Nashville airport. "Bathroom" was the highest request, followed by "balcony." Angie, Carolyn, Jan, Joyce, and I eventually wound up in a tight circle, huddled out on the terrace, staring at the water.

"Uh-maze-ing," Carolyn exhaled as she slumped down in a padded wicker chair, crunching into position.

"Oh, thank you, Lord, thank you, Lord! *Mama Mia.*" Angie whimpered behind her, always mixing her sacred and secular entreaties. "My butt is killing me. Too long in the car!" she whined.

A long silence followed, and someone said, "It's all right now though, isn't it?"

"Uh-huh," someone offered. And then Angie, chronically unfiltered, shouted at the top of her lungs, "This is my house—I live here!" to anyone within earshot at ten o'clock at night for reasons no one understood and never does, for that matter.

Whether it was the comfortable familiarity of the years we've all spent together or just tired indifference, her proud declaration was met with a typical Jan-like, unruffled response: "Thanks for letting us stay, Angie," Jan calmly offered without ever looking away from the surf.

"No problem," Angie quipped, followed by, "I love ya'll," the way a country aunt might talk to her orphaned nieces.

As we sat staring for a while, I noticed how content I felt, happy in the now. Not the now that just passed or the now that was about the next hour. Just the now of Angie being outrageous, Jan being calm, Joyce enjoying the show, and Carolyn being narrative, and all of us breathing together, taking in the vista. I've leaned into these relationships more than I ever could have imagined I would, because I have been convinced that I should, because I made the time to "lean" and to "be." And I've flourished in this provision, all because I finally recognized it for what it is: a gift, entrusted to my care.

Investing consciously in my relationships has made up a big part of my course "correction." Making time for them, feeding them, and enjoying them. Once I let go of what I expected God to do and gently leaned into what He was doing, it started to come together—not in some magic or immediate way but in the old-fashioned, "be patient" way.

I smile as I look at the picture of me and my friends on the beach. I remember a moment toward the end of our first night together on the rooftop terrace. I was feeling drowsy and content as I lounged in the chaise, and after a while my mind formed their voices into music, a symphony. Dramatic swells, hushed whispers, and bursts of laughter rolling into silence. As I started to drift off, with a smile on my face, I heard someone say of me, "She must be having a good dream." I was already one foot into sleep, so I'm sure my lips didn't move when inwardly I answered, "It's not a dream. It's my real life."

• • •

Next to my New Year's photo is one that David had taken of us as a stock photo for an advertisement. We are also leaning into each other, looking a bit more presentable. David is one of the first people I met when I moved to Nashville. Tall, with light Scottish skin and dark wavy hair, he was hard to miss. The fact that he wasn't "taken" was a surprise, as was his generosity, which he demonstrated so graciously when he and another new friend left a basket of "move-in" goodies at the door of my one-room tenement walk-up. I didn't know it when I signed my lease, but it was considered a bad area then. Next to me, a coke dealer. Across the hall, a pimp. David made his concern clear when in the basket, peeking out on top, was an extra door chain. Five moves and eleven years later, we'd both moved in different directions, growing well together and then losing touch for reasons that seem fuzzy to me now. He got busy. I got busy. We formed opinions and new relationships and reasons to be hurt. Eventually, the experiences built up, and we came to that awkward all-or-nothing, get-it-out-on-the-table precipice that long-term relationships tend to come up against. Both being inordinately sensitive, we sidestepped and followed the safer, less-effective course of waiting it out and seeing if something would correct over time. But time, rather than correcting, was a tide that pulled us to different places. I missed him.

When I first came back from the Howard, I called David for dinner. He was someone I'd let slip away. I wasn't sure if I was still in "good standing," but I was sure I didn't want to spend the rest of my life wondering about it. We met for dinner at one of those restaurants that have no inherent romance to them, just a meat-and-three, as they call them in the South. This one was one of our pre-movie favorites at one time because it had his sweet potatoes and my Greek salad. Nestled on opposite sides of the dark burgundy booth, we tentatively caught up over the familiar oak tabletop.

During the time that we'd lost touch, he'd stepped into my dream job as the buyer for an antique store. His job consisted of backwoods auctions, other people's stuff, a budget, and a truck. Being a longtime "garbage picker" myself (a term my mother gave me at seven and one my friends use now to describe my compulsion for thrift stores and consignment shops), I've always had an affinity for other people's discards. It started on Long Island with the annual "trash day" in our neighborhood. On that day only, we could put anything and everything out for the garbage men to haul away. No amount was too much. Washers, dryers, beds, stacks of newspapers from 1922—nothing was forbidden.

It was my favorite day of the year, after my birthday and Christmas. Getting up extra early, I'd start at one end of the street, picking through everyone's junk. Great stuff, things that I couldn't believe anyone would willingly part with. Carefully sorting through it as though it were a mixture of dynamite and fine china, I'd haul home the best and most unusual parcels. A Budweiser lamp, a seafoam-green cracked ashtray, white decorative stones, fake palm branches, a broken blender, a spatula that was burned. I had serious plans for all of it—good plans that would serve not only me but the lonely objects as well. I would have rescued every last one of them if I could have gotten away with it. In my mind, everything could be recycled. Everything could find a purpose. Nothing needed to go to the "dump."

This, of course, left my mother mortified. She knew my obsession with trash day and waited, observing my every move from the window, arms crossed, ready to resist. I wouldn't be three feet back into our yard when I'd see her shadowy figure looming, diffused by the screen of the front door (kind of how I pictured God would appear).

"Go put it all back, Margaret," she'd chide. "I will *not* have other people's trash in my house!"

Frozen in mid-step, I'd sputter out all the reasons I needed the stuff, all the great things I would do with it, all the places I would keep it where she'd never even have to encounter it, but she was immovable. She didn't want a garbage-picker daughter. And this, I believe to her, was much like when she tried to teach the dog not to pass gas in the family room—an ongoing struggle with the impossible that she had to continue out of principle. Head hung low, I'd take it all back to the respective houses, dragging my feet every step of the way, mourning my treasure properly, praying with sick hope that the garbage truck would come and go before I could put it all back in the pile.

I still rubberneck at large trash heaps. I guess I'll always fight that same desire: to take the old and refresh it, the broken and make it functional. In fact, I believe that desire permeates my entire life— even down to my relationships. I love broken things. I feel connected to overlooked treasures. It is my strength and my weakness.

It's my strength in obvious ways, in being able to make something speak that was mute, in seeing gems in broken glass, in wanting to pour myself into restoring things and revitalizing people. But it's my weakness in this way: If I can't control my compulsion to fix and heal, if I can't resist the urge to drag home everything that "needs," then that very same compulsion—however kind or merciful it may seem on any given day—controls me and becomes a liability.

David's relaxed smile in the picture I hold in my hand now is not the one I encountered that night. We tentatively and politely brought each other up to date, as one would with an acquaintance. The conversation was cautious and searching, restrained. I remember chastising myself for allowing this dinner to be put off for far too long. I could tell I had definitely been relegated to the outskirts of his heart. I had been in the inner chamber before, and this was not it.

These things take time, my inner "fixer" assured me. *It still functions. It can be made whole again. It just needs a little—*

Yes, yes, and yes, I thought, but a now-wiser part of me reluctantly acknowledged that just because it is a yes doesn't mean it is a go. I never had been very good at practicing the old adage to accept the things I cannot change. Harder still was accepting that when something can be changed, it doesn't always mean that it should be.

Relationships unearthed my weaknesses and showed me who I was. I either succeeded wildly or failed miserably, the latter eventually being the case with David. In spite of my sincere intention to resurrect our derailed friendship, I fell into old patterns of neglect. I took too long to return a call from him that spring, and I lost him. No amount of trying to make it up to him would fix it. I failed some invisible test, and then, much like his single-wide trailer out in the Tennessee woods, there were no signs of life. I made the trip a few times, with Godivas and apologetic notes in hand, but the result was always the same. No one came to the door. No one acknowledged the journey.

Finally, it was Missy, friend to both of us, who asked me the hard question in the loving way that only true friends can: "Why didn't you return his call, Mag? You really hurt him."

I had no excuse. He was done, and that was that. I had failed. It was the kind of failure I hate the most, the one that has no do-overs. And even worse, it hurt someone I cared about.

The whole thing was reminiscent of a Psychology 101 story I'd heard a hundred times over the years, about the effects of "missing the mark"—the true definition of sin. The father of a small boy taps a nail into the back of his son's bedroom door every time the boy disobeys. After some time, there are many nails. One night, in an effort to demonstrate the concept of forgiveness, the father begins to take the nails out one by one, telling his son that he will forget all that the nails represent and that the two of them will start fresh as if nothing had ever happened. To this the son replies, "But what about the holes?"

Although the nails are gone, the marks they leave stay with the boy. I can't remember what the father says next—as if there could actually be anything comforting to say—other than that grace covers a multitude of mishaps and love covers a multitude of sins. But grace and love working together can enable you to walk through life with nail holes in your soul, still functioning, and, in the best of cases, changed for the better.

As I look once more at the picture of David in my hand, the nail holes puncture me. They point to how reckless I can be with precious things. They serve now as a reminder to be much more careful with people.

Ultimately, I assume they can be a testament and perhaps nothing more. But what does a testament do but remind you to be a little bit better, try a little bit harder, and remember what you're capable of—both good and bad? The picture of David and me next to the picture of me on the beach with my four closest friends can serve me well.

Chapter Twenty-Three

Dribbles of Childhood

Took the afternoon off and went to Home Depot. I never can buy just one thing there. I went in for a hose and, of course, came back with a hose, a lamp, *and* a wireless doorbell. After installing the bell and randomly ringing it for about an hour, I go back up to my pile.

The next box I tackle has some "feel-good" pieces. The first I lift out is the recycled cigar box my sister put together after our last beach visit. Filled with powdery white sand, a crab claw, an old Army man we dug up, and a bobber, it is a miniature ecosphere. I have already set aside a place for it, on my office table. I want to use it as a resting place for my eyes while I work.

I've made it a priority to invite Kate along on my travels more often. If work takes me somewhere exciting or different, I make a place for her. The things that attract her on any given trip are always a mystery to me. Like Seattle. I thought she wanted to go see the Leibowitz photo exhibit. She enjoyed that but even more so the Archie McPhee toy store, where you can get everything from the punching nun to plastic vomit. The creativity of toys and the freedom they represent have always been her detox, I think.

Such was the case the first time I took her along with me for a short jaunt to the beach about eight years ago. I'd found a smaller condo that was available in Blue Mountain Beach on the Gulf. Though it was smaller and tucked back a bit, it had all the things necessary for healing: a view, a path to the sand, and a coffeemaker. I knew that anything other than Kate's daily grind would be a welcome change. Right now she needed a break. Life-transition woes.

As has become my custom whenever I share "my" space at the beach, I got in a day early to set the stage. My first stop was the dollar store, where I bought all the stuff we always wanted as kids. Pails and shovels. Scuba masks, flippers, snorkels, and two pouches of brightly colored diving coins—pirate's treasure. Candy, Twinkies, Sugar Pops, and acrylic paints. I laid them all out on her bed. I stood to the side as she got her first glimpse. Months of worry melted from her countenance. I was once again six and she eleven, waiting for our next adventure.

"Wow," she whispered. The word took a long time to end and was filled with all things both small and grand. She turned to me and asked, "What should we do first?"

"Snorkel and dive for treasure." I said it with an unspoken "of course" as if it were something we did every day.

Off we went in our saggy suits. Children's dive masks pinching our faces, we tossed the coins for one another, waiting for our turns with eyes closed. I'm sure we were a spectacle to anyone who was close enough to see. Two grown women, spasmodically flopping around in the surf with miniature fins and snorkels, shouting, "Ready . . . go!" Sunburn forming on our creased foreheads. Dribbles of childhood flowing between us. Trickery abounding like it always has. Lost in the innocence of it all—free. No adult gear, no adult baggage, no adult worries.

Later we sat on the deck in our shorts and flip-flops, cool drinks in hand. In front of us, drying in the warm dusk, were our water shoes, neatly laid out in a sisterly row. The shoes that kept the crabs from nipping our toes. The shoes that let us walk on the boardwalk without getting splinters. The shoes of freedom, fittingly exhausted by the day. Kate took a picture of them against the surf. She, too, understands their significance.

As she sat back down in the plastic chair, I saw my sister disappear inward for a moment of reflection and emerge again. "What will we do tomorrow?" she asked.

"Anything we want." It was something I said every day we were there.

"Dance around the beach after dark with sparklers?" she piped.

"Yup."

"Eat ice cream for dinner?"

"If you want."

"Keep the back door open so all the cold air escapes?" she asked with a glimmer of rebellion in her eyes.

"We're allowed."

Squinting her eyes against the setting sun, she turned from me to the water. "Thank you for doing this," she said quietly.

"Doing what?" I answered. "This is purely selfish. It's no fun to dive for coins by myself."

Chapter Twenty-Four

The Bug Man

It rains nonstop in Nashville during March. Leaks sprout, roads flood, and weird bugs with thirty thousand legs migrate toward dry land—namely, my house.

Yesterday the bug man came out to take a look at what I was incapable of describing over the phone. A Southern gentleman, Chris approached me as if he was probably used to approaching potentially hysterical women: with authority and reassurance.

"Ma'am, there's nothing this stuff won't take care of, guaranteed," he assured me, holding up his sprayer.

"Really? All right." If he says so. I'm the dream consumer. I believe it all until proven false. "Come take a look at what I was trying to tell you about over the phone," I said, walking to the closet where I'd seen the last offender. I pointed. "This is where I saw one last."

Chris's stance was solid, ready for action. Frowning at the door, canister in one hand, flashlight in the other, he calmly said, "Ms. Becker, just go on and do whatever you would normally do 'round now. I'll take care of it."

Relieved, I happily went back upstairs. Just moments later, I heard the closet door slam.

"Ma'am," the authoritative drawl echoed, "could you come down here for a minute?"

I heard the restraint in his tone. I'm not afraid of bugs generally. I have nothing against them, but this *thing* was just too gross and menacing. I had something against it. When I got to the bottom of the stairs, I saw a white pallor on Chris's face.

"Ma'am, I've never seen anything like that," he began in an expert assessment, pointing over his shoulder with his thumb, back toward the door. "I'm gonna have to take it in to the boys to figure out what it is. That all right?"

My expression mirroring his, I spoke with equal restraint. "Of course. Do whatever you have to do."

"In the meantime, I'm gonna squirt some of this in there for the others. I'm pretty sure it'll kill 'em, but I won't know for sure until I find out what they are."

Others? They? The bug man is spooked. This can't be good.

"Now, if he runs outta there when I open the door, don't worry, I'll catch 'em no matter what, okay?"

"Sure," I said, my wide-eyed glance wandering to the door that framed Chris's figure. "Just let me go upstairs before you do the deed," I instructed.

"Go on, then," he nodded upward solemnly, and I went.

There was a scuffle and then a few curses before I heard the door close for the final time. Chris left, face flushed, clutching a lunch bag of something he described as "freakish" and "one of a kind."

Whatever "they" are, I just wanted them gone because their wriggling bodies were setting up housekeeping in the file cabinet where I keep all my tax records. We are all hard-pressed. I've got to get those records, and they've got to find high ground. It wouldn't be so bad if that was all there was to it, but of course it's all related to satisfying the IRS—and that's enough to give anyone a canker sore all by itself.

I finally called the bug man when I found one of their dead bodies in my "Investments" folder. An insult. It was one of the areas I had been most diligent since writing down goals like "I will save money and find someone to help me invest it productively." That was just over a decade ago, and my investment advisor says he's never seen anyone save so much so quickly. He asked me what my technique was. I laughed. There is no technique. I just stopped spending money on things I didn't really need, things that had no long-term value. My fear of becoming a very elderly hash slinger at Bob's Big Boy didn't hurt either.

All in all, there still are a few areas of my spending that need trimming. Phone service seemed pretty high the last few times I reviewed my bill. And the random stops to the ATM, which I don't keep track of at all—they're a black hole. I have no idea where all that cash goes.

Budget, budget. Pull it in a little tighter. Spend money on only the necessary things. Be serious about my responsibility to take care of myself now and in the future. Practice diligence and expertise and courage—like the bug man.

Chapter Twenty-Five

True North

Max has taken to the new house well. He has already found his favorite spot, lying on the air conditioning/heater grate in the living room. It serves all his needs. He can see out the door, get cooled down, and harass those who walk by, if need be. He hasn't wanted to be up here in my room while I sort. Too hot.

I found a picture of him predawn, in the surf, from our second visit to the Gulf together. It fell from that year's journal this morning, and I relived wonderful memories of our life together as I slipped it back into the entry that it belongs with:

> *I sat huddled against the dunes last night when I got in.*
> *It was dark and the wind pressed the waves into elongated*
> *apex patterns. Max leaned up against me, blocking the wind.*
> *Although it was only his second time to the beach, his posture*
> *spoke generations of breeding. A golden retriever—he was meant*
> *to be here.*
>
> *The rest of the gang went grocery shopping, but I couldn't*
> *bear to be in a car for another minute. If stress had shape and*
> *form, anyone looking at me there would see a wisp of stress smoke*

wafting out of my brain and gently blowing eastward. I could feel it leaving me, sense it subsiding. I feel this way every single time I arrive at the beach.

My eyes focused on nothing in particular—not the water, not the sky, not the shadowy sand. It all just coalesced there like a breathing entity, like it was the energy source for all of existence, the wizard behind the curtain.

As I felt myself open up, the space the stress had left filled with equal amounts of wonder. Wonder at the fact that I am here at all. Wonder about the past few years and how many incredible moments they've contained. Wonder about how much of my life has shifted and come into focus and how much remains to be determined. Wonder about how life change came from the simple act of putting crayon to paper and imagination to use.

I walked down to the shoreline, tossing the sticks that Max brought me along the way. He never tires of bringing me things. A ball, a stick, a sock, a stuffed animal—there's always an offering in his mouth when he first greets me at the front door at home.

I'd say Max is the poster boy for my new life, representing the changes I wanted but whose presence I feared. He's the picture of the commitment side of change. How well I remember when he came to me by way of two well-meaning friends. They watched me forge my way through a series of bouts with loneliness and responded with an "intervention." I went to their house for Christmas dinner. Came home with a dog.

The initial introduction went great. I was instructed to hold out my arms and close my eyes. A soft furry ball was placed in my arms like an infant, curled up in the crook of my elbow. When I opened my eyes, a puppy gently stretched to my face and licked my chin. I was a goner.

Of course, I'd wanted a golden retriever forever. According to my life stories, I am counting on growing old with one. I just

*didn't expect one then. My "plan" was to get him next year if it
turned out that I could stay home more.*

So much for plans.

*The next day, I drove home on the interstate, puppy crying
and trying to wrap himself around my neck like a fox stole. We
arrived unceremoniously at my postage-stamp-sized front yard.*

*"This is your new house, buddy," I baby-talked to him as we
tumbled out of the car, dog paraphernalia spilling every which way.*

*He looked around and whimpered again. If it is possible for a
puppy to look concerned, he certainly did.*

*I felt sad for him. I have no idea what gave me the notion
that he would possibly understand that his future was bright, that
he would get treats and pets and lambskin rugs. He had no idea he
had just walked into his nirvana with an animal freak who works
at home.*

*And then I tried to remember what to do next. What did I do
the last time I had a puppy? My skin did that contraction shrink-
wrap motion, the same way it does when I have that recurring
nightmare where I'm an adult, standing in front of my high school
locker again, books in hand, with the terrible realization that I
never graduated high school because I missed too many gym classes
or didn't take my trig final. I quickly indexed my past and realized
I'd never trained, raised, or been responsible for a puppy—my
parents did it all! What was I thinking?*

*At that very moment, Max came to face me, worried little
furrow on his baby head. We both stared at each other that way for
a long time. I can't vouch for him, but I know I felt overwhelmed.
All of a sudden, having a dog seemed like an impossible, implausi-
ble thing for me to do.*

*And besides that, the timing seemed off. His presence meant
that I wouldn't be able to leave home for long periods of time. The
responsibility of him meant a loss of freedom—or, perhaps on a*

deeper level, a loss of a choice. I knew that once I was attached, I would be committed. There would be no more long absences and, more specifically, no ability to change my mind and take back all the internal shifts I'd recently made.

And then the other issue: my loneliness. Was it that obvious? To accept the dog was to accept the assessment too. I hadn't been lonely in years. In fact, my biggest people issues had to do with getting away from them for a rest. But now, in pursuit of "chapter 2" in my life, I was out of my usual element, and I was lonely. But I was capable and resourceful! And besides, how much difference would a dog make? After all, a dog is an animal. It can't converse with you. It can't replace humans.

As I tossed Max the final shard of driftwood tonight, I felt guilty for my initial reactions back then. My dog has brought me comfort. And no, he can't talk; but frankly, right now in my life I'd trade unconditional devotion for a good verbal exchange any day.

Yes, I've had to make some adjustments. I've had to commit to my course of staying home more. I've had to lose my penchant for a spotless house. I've had to learn how to cut dog toenails, clean dog ears, give medication in tricky ways, and read dog sign language. And I've had to accept the generous love of two close friends and a gift that required me to be vulnerable and admit need. But it's been worth it—difficult, but so right.

As Max trotted ten feet ahead of me back to the boardwalk and my friends, I realized what a constant reminder he is of all the change that has swept through my life, both comfortable and risky. Zigzagging back and forth, chasing scents and seaweed lifted by the wind, Max's gait is metered, slow, and deliberate. He carves a trail that mirrors my own: controlled chaos with a pattern formed only by instinct. I'm sure that to someone coming down the beach later in our footsteps, our path will look messy and untamed. But as we walked it, I gauged its median: True North, without a doubt.

Now, only two years later, I can't even imagine my life without a beautiful little presence around to fill the house. It's a simple comfort to have another living thing to interact with. It slows the day, too, forcing me to take it all in. I have to stop to tend to him. He needs to walk, he needs to play, and I need to take my little breaks.

It has been perfect, starting first thing in the morning. More reliable than any clock, every day between five thirty and six, I feel a paw nudging the side of my bed. I open my eyes to the only wake-up alarm better than National Public Radio: Max, ball lightly held in his jaw, ears up with expectation, wagging his tail so hard it fans me. I never would have predicted what a joy it would be to wake to that.

Chapter Twenty-Six

The Provision
of His Presence

Perhaps one of my favorite things about my new house is its location. It's close to everything and everyone significant to me. When I was traveling constantly, all I wanted to do when I got home was retreat. I didn't want to see another person or carry on a conversation. My former house allowed for that. Off the beaten path, nestled in a hillside, it was a hike for anyone. I liked it that way. But this is a different time of life. My life is about community now. I am in community. I want to be around people. There's space for that because I'm not constantly worn out. It is a clear picture to me of God's faithful provision.

On any given night, I can have up to ten people around my table. Tonight Valerie is stopping by on her way home to her family. We'll sit on the porch and shoot the breeze. She is always an interesting visitor because she's bold. If she's ever been afraid, I don't know of it. Her Bible study was one of my first entry points back into "civilization" eleven years ago.

She named the small group, comprised of Bible school graduates and scrappers, The Agitators. Valerie would call it a "meeting," a "collective." Just the girls, it was determined, no spouses. We met that first Wednesday night, unsure of what The Agitators were or how close to "real" we would be allowed to journey. As we watched Valerie's husband cart the kids off to Chuck E Cheese's, the anticipation was palpable.

That night, Valerie worked her Martha Stewart magic on us. Quiche, phyllo, and a gourmet salad. All made by hand. All after a long day at the office. Even the kitchen was neat. I raised the question I think we were all considering: "How is it that some women can run a corporation, raise children and dogs, be a good wife, and make Christmas decorations from grass, looking fabulous through it all?"

All heads turned to Valerie.

"Don't ask me," she said in her best sound-clueless voice. "Anyone can do it!"

"Yeah, right," the rest of us managed in one form or another. Not just anyone.

As I looked around the table, I realized what a unique and powerfully determined lot we were. *Not just anyone.* In this group, feminine strength bloomed in abundance. We were stubborn survivors, running at times on only spit and wishes. An unlikely demographic of the spirit.

The Agitators became a clandestine forum where the blunt questions that arise from life experience were laid bare. It was a reverse debate of sorts. Instead of trying to prove our individual points, we examined individual questions as a group, each of us offering our meager understanding. Topics ranged far and wide. Prayer, for example. The mechanics of it all. The act of praying: Does it move God to move, or do we every once in a while fall into some eternal synchronicity that results in our becoming a part of His mysterious movement? True responsibility: What are we truly and undeniably responsible for in our relationships? Are we necessary for

God's matrix to function correctly? Is our compliance necessary for His will to be accomplished on Earth?

No one reigned over the group with the absolute answer. No one waited at the end of a discussion with the buzzer underhand: Ready, set, "right" or "wrong." CEOs, administrators, producers, graphic artists, writers—we were an amalgamation of thought. Our church affiliations ranged from Pentecostal to Catholic. We were a myriad of talents, and lifetimes of experience.

And all that experience is what drew us together. Hard experience—when preconceived notions don't align with true life. When you pray very hard and sincerely and someone dies of cancer. When it's logical to walk away from a marriage, but you stay because you believe in the sanctity of vows and the effort that must ensue. Experience versus expectation. Truth versus reality. Eternity versus Polaroid moments. All tiny trails that led us to Valerie's.

Not because we were looking for answers—I am convinced of that—but because we were looking for the tattered accounting of nomads, the limited enlightenment of collective understanding. We were looking for others like ourselves who were willing to accept the gaps and the mysteries that run parallel with supposed absolutes. We were looking for a blank template, a safe place where we could lay out our questions and tangles in temporary patterns, gauging how they fit against conscience and deity. "How does this work for you?" could have easily been the question asked at each gathering. "How do you rectify this?"

Scripture reference upon cross-reference, experience upon experience, we built. Topic by topic, we dressed each other's wounds in the most dignified of ways: without pity. I think we all silently agreed on that. No pity. No remorse. The truth was that we were all still here. Still believing. Still relying on the spiritual compass that set our course in the first place. And our faith in that compass—no matter where or what the aberrations—is what allowed each of us to get up close to it, to test it, to inspect it. Like children with magnifying glasses examining things just out of reach, we boosted one another to the task. We probed and examined. We mused and often came to no conclusions.

God Himself was not questioned, per se; our understanding of Him was. I believe it is a mature premise to ask questions of your faith without feeling like an infidel. Surely faith is up to the test and God is not bothered by mortal curiosities. To be given minds that toy with riddles and revel in mysteries is confirmation enough of God's design of us. We can ask and seek because we were created to.

The collective that Valerie started, this invitation to journey in the questions, has been one of the greatest gifts in my post-"coming to" life. In true form, I am sure that at some point tonight, she will lob one out there for everyone to debate, and just as quickly as we all get into it, she'll shift the subject to the last movie she's seen, just to mix it up.

These are the moments I love most: the chatter of community, the banter of old friends, and the provision of His presence expressed in His people.

Chapter Twenty-Seven

Between the "Was" and the "Not Yet"

The mosquitoes are wicked here. They even *look* menacing, with their jet-black spindly legs banded with white. You never feel them on you, but after they've had their fill, you scratch for days. For the amount of bites I get daily, I must be filet mignon to them. This morning I sprayed my entire body with repellent. On my way out to the backyard with Max, coffee cup in hand, I was of immediate interest to the vermin—and then just harassed. They didn't like this at all, and they showed me as much when they had a feast on the one area I didn't think to spray: my rear.

The mornings here have a rhythm to them. They start the same time they have for the past decade, and they include all the same props as well: coffee cup, Bible, journal, reading glasses (recently added), and sticky notes. I use the sticky notes to record any bits of revelation that come my way as well as the questions I have. My Bible looks like a Mardi Gras float, and my pastor is officially avoiding me.

For a little over a year now, I've been studying the journey of the Israelites out of Egypt. I've read it countless times over the course of my life, but in light of the past decade's traverse, it's spoken to me differently. It's helped me make some sense of delay and silence.

It was early last spring when I finally saw the truth of their journey as it applied to me. Bundled up in the driveway of my old house, tossing Max the ball on and off, I huddled over my tiny travel Bible, specs resting on the bulb of my nose. I'd read it so many times, I was tempted to rush through, but then something different poked its head up among the familiar: *They were never lost.*

I don't know why I always had this overt or subliminal impression that they wandered in the desert for forty years because they were lost. I knew they were being tested and that they failed many of those tests, leaving God angered. But I had never recognized the value of the delay in their final steps toward the land they were to possess: the land flowing with milk and honey. I believe they were delayed because had they stepped foot into that land without the proper strengths in place, they could not have sustained themselves there. It's the difference between entering a land and possessing a land. They needed so many things first, like absolute disciplined assurance that what God had spoken to them was true, no matter what contradicted it—and the courage that comes along with that kind of conviction.

Early in their journey they celebrated, composing songs of praise and recalling what God had done for them. But not long after, they began complaining. Though they knew that God had laboriously and gloriously removed them from Egypt *and* miraculously provided, right down to the parting of the Red Sea, the experience of it all did not sustain them on their long journey through the desert. Yet we see from the account in the book of Numbers that what they perceived as God's *punishment* of them was really God's *pleasure* on them. We know this because when God got fed up with it all, He spoke and told them that He indeed would do everything they asked for and that His acquiescence would be *His displeasure:* "How long [must I endure] this evil community that keeps complaining about Me? . . . Tell them: As surely as I live, declares the LORD, I will do to you exactly as I heard you say. . . .You will know My displeasure."[16]

The journey they had been experiencing up until then—the one that was by faith, by daily intuitive response to God's provision of water and manna, a pillar of cloud by day and fire by night, and the direction of a humble, loving leader, Moses—was God's pleasure on them. That, too, jumped out at me. It pleased Him to have them utterly dependent on Him so that He could show the people His love for them through providing the many things they needed to thrive when they reached His ultimate destination for them.

It's what has been happening to me over the past decade: an intuitive journey, initiated by a prodding, a leading from God. I walked as the Israelites walked, in the strength of new promise. I, too, was tired at the middle, wondering if the daily provision was my prize or punishment. Any peace or assurances I received were hard-won—not that I had to wrestle them from God's hand, but rather, I wrestled them from my own fatalist predisposition.

Reviewing some of the journals I am packing away in my new "testimonial" room to God's faithfulness has taken me back to some of the things I experienced and felt after I returned from the Howard.

What a slap in the face. Came home to ice, frozen pipes, and malfunctioning pilot lights. Real life.

It took me hours just to sort through my messages and my mail. In the middle of a two-page call-back list, I chanted under my breath, "Remember the Howard, remember the Howard." It worked—at least for the moment.

I forced myself to go down to the middle school to run around the track. Snow was freshly fallen. The entire city stops when there is even a whisper of it, so the place was deserted. Around and around I ran—in snow boots. And all the unhappy antagonistic voices were shouting at me the whole way—about how I was going to twist my ankle, get shin splints, form ice in my lungs, blah, blah, blah. I was trying to be tough, but by the third lap, the voices started to make sense and the scenery was about as exciting as a six-hour layover in Timbuktu.

So I stopped. I was not winded. I was not even tired in the least. I was just plain bored.

Still, I suspect out of sheer stubbornness and defiance of the Defeatist Choir, I started again. I lumbered around until I made my thirty-five minutes and then rewarded myself with a promise that I would never do this again—not here, anyway, and not in snow boots.

I began a new discipline after my abrupt reentry into reality. I kept a calendar on which I wrote only brief daily descriptions of God's faithfulness to me. It forced me to see the "bread from heaven and the water from the rock"[17] every day. It helped and continues to as I keep it up. But my journals over the years remind me of the many times I felt lost and afraid.

Lay awake for too long. Moved my worry session downstairs to the living room, where I quietly panicked for about three hours on the couch.

Wide-eyed, staring at the moon, I reviewed my every move of the last few years, starting with my present worries, reaching back to my epiphany at the beach. For a time—a short time that seemed like an eternity—I asked myself if I did the right thing.

I corrected course.

I dreamed big.

I defined direction.

I followed direction.

Fine. Then why am I up at 3:00 a.m. worrying? I had peace when I decided to redirect the focus of my time. I had peace when I pursued other goals. I even had peace with the shift in finances that comes when you start a new venture.

But this is taking so long to take shape. Too long. Scary long. I am in that middle part of the redirection, I think—the part that is undefined and dark. I keep moving, but I don't feel any shift in place. I'm rowing, but I have nothing to navigate by, other than the original prompting to get in the boat and go to the other side.

What other side? Where is that? It's vague. Somewhere "over there."

It's getting rough out here, and I don't have a sense of strong guidance. I'm like the disciples crossing the lake when the storm came up. I know that my journey, like theirs, originated with Christ's prompting. I believe I heard correctly to venture with Him from the comfortable to the unknown. I believe He agreed to come with me in the "boat." But, like them, when it gets too dark and rough, I wonder if I got it all wrong, although in my gut I know that I didn't. I really do. I can't return; that doesn't feel right. I must keep going, but that doesn't feel comfortable either. It's this middle change that I did not account for. How could I have missed it?

Going somewhere means leaving somewhere.

Choosing something means choosing against other things.

Gaining something means losing something else.

And between the old and new—the "was" and the "not yet"— there exists only one thing: a very frightening journey called faith. It is stripped of the usual comforts. It comes in one color: dark. It offers one amenity: catharsis.

And perhaps the most significant truth—the one that super- sedes my senses, the one that circumnavigates my obstacles, the one

I should be focusing on now—is who makes the journey with me, who ordained it, and who is in the boat.

I remind myself of Jesus' disposition in Luke's gospel account. While the storm raged, Jesus slept. Just as the journey across the raging water became terrifying to His disciples, He was at rest, fully confident of His ability to deliver them safely on the other side.

I find this truth challenging as the moon begins to fade into the dawn. With it comes repentance as I mix my own personal history with the best measure of faith I can muster. After all, if Jesus is sleeping, maybe I should be too.

As my little boat has crossed safely time and again, I have come to appreciate how practicing this kind of trust and intuitive faithful following helped me prepare for what was on the other side, in my own "Promised Land." And I have learned that all lands flowing with milk and honey come with their share of giants.

Max is about four feet away from me on his side in the grass, puffing from exertion. The tattered tennis ball is firmly clamped in his teeth, and the sun has finally risen over the billboard that sits just beyond my alley on Twelfth Avenue.

I can hear the distant thump of a subwoofer in a passing Cutlass Supreme. I know that to some, this setting might look like punishment, but to me it is the promise. It is flowing with all things sweet and nourishing: the milk of community, the sweetness of fulfillment and significance, the manna of God's presence.

I am happy here, of that I am sure—all except for the mosquitoes.

Chapter Twenty-Eight

Reckless Trust

I remember sitting outside on the deck one night at the Howard under a moonless sky. It was freezing, but the air was still. Bundled up on the wooden chair, I leaned my head back and studied the heavens. So many stars in the sky. The lights showed themselves much more clearly against the absolute darkness. Nothing competed with them, no other light sources.

So much of the past eleven years has been like that spiritually—hearing things I'd tuned out, seeing things I'd missed, noticing the things I'd never noticed before—because I'd stopped looking at everything the same way. I changed angles and positions. I stopped waiting for the "perfect" light to make all things plain. I started to enjoy the imperfection of it all. People, relationships, me, nature, work, just life itself. I stopped focusing on what "wasn't" and started to see what "was."

One year while on my annual beach retreat, I wrote these words under "Spiritual": "To become more gracious, realistically, in a way I cannot claim as my own or take pride in." It took bravery to write it, because I know how these things are accomplished. By trial. By fire. By deconstruction. This goal would be met by my own undoing, my own loose ends coming to the surface.

What a release I've had. I've stopped looking to people to meet my deepest needs and have found that I've enjoyed people more than ever before. When they come through on any level, I am delighted. When they miss, I can rest inside. The latest accusation from my friendly naysayers concerning my spirituality is that I am skewed in my thinking, that I err on the side of grace.

What a lovely place to err. A gift, in fact. May I always be guilty.

* * *

This year has been one of letting go. Somewhere in my life, a strong association was made for me: "letting go" with "failure and loss." The connection is strong. It feels almost absolute, like a linear, moral teaching.

Letting go means that you couldn't carry the ball. You couldn't complete the task. You failed. Letting go has lain on my heart like shame. *Not this* _____ enough or *not that* _____ enough. Not enough, so what to do? Let go. Let go and mark the day, the place, and the time. Mark it with the admittance—failure. The realization—loss. I am sure that is why it has been so hard to let go at all. Incorrect associations. Wrong assumptions.

When did it become so important to win? When did completing a task become more valuable than the journey itself? When did the end become more important than the refining process? We have forgotten the reverence for the work itself.

Reverence for the process. Reverence for the passage. Respect for the sensitivity that is required to determine the path, to know when to turn right, to know when to turn left. To know when to let go and call it complete—even if everyone who looks on does not see the same conclusion, hear the same command to abandon.

Instead, we fail, and we feel shame. Shame is a compulsory emotion, driving us all deeper into ourselves, sending us scrambling for cover. It breeds trust. Reckless trust. Absolute trust. Abandonment to things immeasurable and at times unproven. Bravery. Pursuit that sometimes leads us to the end of ourselves in very public ways.

And to find your own end, your limitations—why does that seem like a wall? Why doesn't it seem like another road or another opportunity? Another journey not yet taken?

When I let go of my preconceived notions of what God would and would not do, I felt a paradigm shift inside. Suddenly, I was no longer in control—God was. He was free to express Himself however He pleased. I was free to experience Him incarnate, personified, in living forms that can be detected by the senses.

What probably seemed like failure to some—my saying no more, my refusal to just "go along"—became a joyful, refining journey for me. I excused myself from the need to be perfect, the need to please. The end result was a more spontaneous journey, one where God met me in many fresh ways—many of which took my breath away.

At certain times, it's been almost like a sensory overload. I've encountered Him in so many diverse places that it is overwhelming. And that recognition of Him is akin to having clear, unencumbered vision, seeing through hearts and walls, looking at creation from the inside out.

When I stopped "expecting" to see or predefining what I would see, I began to truly see. When I let go of what I thought I knew, I found out that I knew very little. At another time, that would feel like failure. Failure in applying myself to my faith. Failure to understand all things in a timely fashion. Failure to propagate "the answers." Failure to keep up the status quo.

This year, it was just new. All new. All undetermined. All fresh. Alive. The core tenets of my faith remained, but the nuances, the expressions—they took on many facets. When the pompous illusions went away, true form emerged. It is much more sturdy and sure, this form. It does not require my approval to function. It asks nothing of my strength. It only asks, for perhaps the millionth time, for my trust: childlike and open, flexible, waiting for the surprise.

Chapter Twenty-Nine

Emancipation

I found a bag this afternoon containing some schoolwork from my years in New York. I think my parents gave it to me when I left for college. In it was a picture of the United States that I'd drawn in the second grade. It contained only two states—New York and Florida—the only states I recognized as real then, because everyone I knew was either living in New York or retiring to Miami. I got a B on it.

Along with my brightly colored map was a picture of me in front of my high school locker. It sent a shiver up my spine, not because of my high school experience but because of the one that came after it.

My parents had decidedly different strategies for my life. My mother was my dreamer, never setting boundaries, reinforcing my pursuit of the moment, be it music or writing, no matter how impossible it might seem to make a living at it. She would scarcely offer any alternative advice other than what would help me accomplish those dreams.

My father "rooted" for me in all the same areas, but ultimately he was the voice of reason, prefacing his suggestions with comments like, "I don't mean to rain on your parade, but . . ." His was the voice of practicality: "Work at the phone company. They've got good benefits." "Go down to Sears. They have a great stock program." And my least favorite of all: "Get some secretarial skills." Nothing against all of that. It is all good and respectable work, challenging and creative in some cases—not to mention sane—and smart. In fact, right about now in my life, a pension is looking as desirable as a never-been-married Dr. Bodybuilder with a fat 401K.

But at twenty, I didn't want to come to my senses. It seemed premature. That was the year I was working as a check encoder at a bank part-time, trying to save enough to go back to college. The money I managed to make barely covered my gas for the trip back and forth to the job. It was a never-ending cycle of frustration. No matter how I tried, I could not seem to get my life to "go."

I know that my father was concerned. I was in a crying jag at one point for months straight. Like the Holly Hunter character in the old movie *Broadcast News*, every morning I'd wake at six so that I could get out of bed and get the crying out of my system. I'd allow myself about twenty minutes of it, along with desperate prayers and pleas for God to "do something." After I was finished, I'd drag myself down to the coffeemaker, face red and swollen, head down, shoring up to face another day. My father would use those moments to make his suggestions. I knew that on some level, he was right, but the thought of finding another cubicle in a different dungeon to tether myself to felt like a death sentence—dental plan or no dental plan.

He and I would talk about it often and sometimes argue. After a while, we came to a détente: I would enroll in the adult courses that were taking place in my old high school, starting with typing.

There's something about going back to your old high school as an adult. I can't explain why, but it is just not pleasant—at least it wasn't for me. The first night of class, I parked my car in the same spot where I used to park my old '64 Dodge Polara. I made the same dreaded walk through the parking lot and around to the front of the building. I opened the left side of the double doors and got my first whiff of that musty stationer's smell: paper products, books, and dusty upholstery.

I slid my feet across the rubber mat between the first set of doors and the second set, got the same shock as my electrified grip made contact with the steel handle, pulled the door open, and stepped onto the polished floor.

I wanted to vomit right then and there. I was already late because I'd sat in my car at Burger King forcing myself to accept the fact that I was going to learn to type. I was going to be a secretary at Sears. I was going to let go of all those stupid notions that I could do music. I was going to, dare I say it, give up and conform.

It was the right thing to do. It was. That's what I told myself as I ate my fries slowly, taking at least six tiny bites on every fry, deliberately wasting time, hoping I'd "come to" way after the start time of the class. I stayed at Burger King until the last ketchup packet was drained, taking my last reason to dillydally with it. That, coupled with the disappointment my father would surely feel toward me, made me start the car and go.

By the time I got there, it was twenty minutes past the start time. The school was deserted. I headed toward Room 101. I knew it well. It was right next to the locker where I had spent my entire high school career. I knew 101 had thirty typewriters in it. I'd heard their fastidious clicking for four years. Back then, I used them as markers of time, sporadic seconds ticking by in spurts. Tick, tick, tick-tick-tick. Fast, energetic bursts of liberation, counting down the moments to the time when I was "free" and cut loose to live my "real" life. With the sound of every keystroke, I was inwardly relieved that my real life was not starting in that room, learning to type.

I could hear the seconds ticking off again as I tiptoed down the hall this time, careful not to alert anyone of my presence, leaving myself an out to the very last minute. I could hear the instructor saying, "In this class, you will be required to blah, blah, blah . . ."

The rollers clicked as the whole class loaded up their first piece of paper. My heart was racing, my hands shaking. I willed my quiet feet to take me right up to the door, where I leaned on my tiptoes to peek in. I saw nothing different than I expected to see, really. Women poised at massive gray machines. All eyes fixed on the front of the class.

Some of the expressions reminded me of my own: general desperation wrapped in distaste. One woman noticed me, turning her gaze slightly to see my head framed in the tiny window. Her face was without emotion, head cocked slightly to the right. Her hands were folded and in her lap, short fingers with long tapered red nails, a gold ring on every finger. Something about her and her posture, something about the rest of the class—something was just beige, colorless, monochromatic life-draining.

I came down off my toes and felt the strangest emotions flood over me. Tears welled up in my eyes as I started to laugh. I was sure that right there, at the door of Room 101, steps away from my locker, I was having a nervous breakdown! The more I laughed, the harder I cried, until something even stranger happened. My feet, as if a separate entity, turned me around in military fashion and began making their way back down the hallway to the front door. The tears subsided, and under my breath I acknowledged the emancipation to myself: "I'm not going in there. I'm not going in there." I said it over and over, emphasizing different words in the sentence. "*I'm* not going in there." "I'm *not* going in *there!*" "I'm not *going* in there." With each recitation, I was a little lighter, a little freer, like a spell had been broken.

I made it out to my car and began driving aimlessly out to the east end of Long Island. I didn't know where or to what. I just knew that I was not going in there.

If I'd only known then what I know now: that the entire world would be based on computers and typing. That learning to hit the "6" without looking away from your screen would be a big plus. That stop-offs and delays in life are not necessarily ends in and of themselves. Sometimes there is a greater plan that needs a few skills, a few accessories, in order to be accomplished.

It's me and the Israelites again. Delays, preparation, dread. I didn't have it in me then to endure, although I wish I would have. I come perilously close to ordering the Mavis Bacon—or whatever it's called—typing course. I've been bumbling around for years, trapped in my two-fingered technique.

Looking back at the photograph of me and that locker, I have regrets. Typing skills would be nice right about now. In fact, if I had to do it all over again, I'd . . .

Nah. I *still* wouldn't go in there.

Chapter Thirty

The Love of the Game

Been at my desk for hours now trying to organize. My office in this house is in the back. It overlooks the deck and the yard. I have purposefully kept it bare, with just a desk that sits on casters. I want the freedom to change positions, face east or south depending on my mood.

I used to work for hours straight, forgetting to eat or break. I'd put my head down at nine thirty, look up and see four. Max has changed all that. He is a built-in timer. About four times a day, he pads down the hall, ball in mouth, and sits like a show dog, ears perked. His tail swishes on the floor as he waits for me to notice him. It's my cue that it's been too long, too serious, too much. I take a break every time because I have learned that if I play more in life, I am better at life.

So we go outside, and I jump around in ways that are sure to someday break my ankle. I breathe like a monster, threaten him, and bellow on in my mother's threat voice, "You'd better!" Neither he nor I know what he'd "better" do. It just serves to ignite the atmosphere.

The dollar store is around the corner from me. It takes all my will not to go in there every day. I went to buy cleaning solvent when I first moved in, and I came back with a big green ball for Max. It's our new game—soccer. Even though the ball has long been deflated, I jig from foot to foot, showing him my fancy technique, and he reciprocates. I am sure it's amusing for the people in the apartment complex across my yard, but I don't care. I need to play. I love to play. And like anything else as an adult, I have to make time for it.

I think adult play makes cultures healthy in many ways. It's a truth I saw lived in Africa, one I was reminded of yesterday when I put away one of my Africa journals.

> *I've made it to Ghana, Africa, with World Vision. Hot. Hot. Hot.*
>
> *Morning started early here. I was shocked awake by the sound of a chicken—somebody's prized possession—singing out. Poor thing. It doesn't know it's on borrowed time, but I know better. In Kenya, the townspeople honored us with a feast—their one ewe goat—speared through by a stick and roasted over an open fire. Forsaking etiquette, I said I was "fasting" that day. It was the only out, and once I claimed it, the rest of my colleagues had no excuse. We sat by the skinless form, them scowling and choking down goat. I was never so happy about hunger pangs.*
>
> *The thought of it made me wince as I turned over in my cot and squinted at my watch. Five thirty. I propped myself up on my elbow, trying to tune in to the unfamiliar sounds coming through the window. I could hear muted voices of children and men calling out to one another in signals. Adult laughter and the dull thump of something else, something a little familiar.*
>
> *Everything I do in this room echoes through the whole of this concrete structure, where the rest of the team from World Vision is sleeping, so I raise myself up carefully, trying not to creak the springs on the bed.*

The days have been long but different from the first time I came over to Africa. That initial visit was difficult. There were so many children frail and sickly, not yet helped by the aid that World Vision brings.

I remember how I tried to steel myself against it then, knowing that if I felt even the least of it all, I would be incapacitated in a pit of emotion. I tried that the first few days, but it didn't work. I knew that in order to help feed these kids, I had to feel it all— even if it was more horrifying than anything I'd known before.

I learned so much on that trip and, as a result, found a way to bring aid to thousands of the African people. This trip is a bit more lighthearted. The projects we are visiting this round are in better shape. The country itself doesn't feel quite as oppressed. In fact, I'd say there is a lightness to these people overall.

The voices in the distance remind me that I know nothing of how the other side of the world lives, and although I wrapped my sweater around my ears, the thump and cock-a-doodle-do still bled through until curiosity got the better of me. I pulled my cot to the wall, which had a window about six feet off the ground. I stood up on the thin mattress with precarious balance and peered out the opening.

It was a soccer game: grown men playing soccer on a patch of gray dirt. How unlike the U.S., where it's a chore to get up first thing in the morning to go work out or do anything physical, for that matter—even in air conditioning. Here it was 5:30 a.m., and these guys were playing a friendly game of soccer in ninety-degree heat. It's not like they needed to lose weight or even that they would have pent-up energy. They barely get one meal a day. They work the fields for a living. Why were they playing?

The answer arrived in lush, African-tinged English later that day. The chief's response was simple, almost profound: "Dey luv futball!" he declared as if it were the most obvious truth. "It is what dey do for demselves, jou see? Dey haf no ele-tricity, so dey do little et night. Mos nights, dere is little actibity et dusk, and den eberyone goes to sleep. Duh firs ting in duh morning, dey play. It is cool den." He offered the explanation with his hands out to the sides, shrugging as though it should be obvious.

"Dee Amehrikans don do dis—no?" he smiled, eyebrows raised.

"Not exactly," was the best answer I could come up with. No, not truly for the love of the game. And certainly not when it isn't convenient. Not if it includes getting up at five to make the kickoff—at least not most of us, anyway.

But what a wonderful thought. What if we all played just to play, just for the love of play? I wonder if we'd be more settled. Laugh more, sleep better, have better relationships. Understand our kids a little better—help them understand that being an adult is like being a kid, only with resources and freedom. That holistic, healthy fun is not something you can have just when you are under twenty, or something that comes to adults only through too much alcohol and high-priced toys.

In all my life planning, I'd forgotten about "the love of the game." How wonderful it is just to have fun. Just to play because you still love to play. To actually make time in your day to play. To find the things you like to do, however foolish someone else might find them, and just do them—because it feels good. Because it seems right. Because it feeds your soul in a way that few things do—without agenda, without boundaries, with imagination.

It was the next day when I—newly freed—was approached by some village girls. In one of their hands was a small stone. With it they traced a grid on the ground that resembled a hopscotch board. A combination of charades and practice runs gave me the rundown. The overall goal? Not to be the odd man out, which I managed to be every time.

We played until the seam between us disappeared and I became just another playmate to be included, to be beaten, to pass the time with. And in the language of play, we ultimately parted, without fanfare or remorse. The days are endless when spent like that. The games will begin again tomorrow. It is part of life. And I will be there to play.

Chapter Thirty-One

Being Available

One of the hardest things about moving here was leaving Lillian, my next-door neighbor. When I began to shift my focus, I asked God to "highlight" the things He wanted me to devote myself to. Lillian was positively yellow.

I've known her since she was born, and I've prayed for her that long as well, but my travel schedule did not allow for me to become as good of a neighbor as I wished. When I stuck around a little more *and* got Max, Lillian started to come over more, often spending the afternoon on my couch either entertaining Max as I worked or speed-talking to me about her day.

It was a time of day I looked forward to and, in many instances, had to use my "yes" template for. As life goes, the times when Lillian had big news or needed some company would happen at approximately 4:40 p.m. on a day when somebody absolutely *had to have* something by five. I'd weigh it all out in my head as she'd begin her soliloquy. It was a mental tug-of-war for about two minutes, and then I'd remember my joy, my flow, my responsibility—the ultimate and overarching one—in this life. Listening to Lillian was not only my pleasure but my calling. The pen would go down, the keyboard would stop clicking, and I would enter in. She was more important than any deadline or business function. I was called to her, and she was gifted to me.

The day I told her I was moving, I took her to the new house and showed her the room that I had set aside for her with her parents' blessing. Long weekends, summer vacation, or just "whenever," this was her place. I knew we would both miss the casual stop-bys, but now that she was getting older, the prolonged dinner or hang time seemed even more valuable to me.

I came across a picture of myself at Lillian's age the other day. I barely remember thirteen; in fact, the only record I have of it is that Catholic confirmation picture in which I look like a disgruntled Danny Bonaduce in drag, squinting into the sun on my front step. What I *do* remember was that my two front teeth were too big and I sweat all the time. Life was dazzling and scary. I felt older and younger. I was miserable. Not like Lillian, who is so much more comfortable with herself, a "creative" to the core. Cool and kind and smart.

I have a friend from New York who visits often and uses Lillian's room. On her last visit, we sat at dinner together and she and Lillian bargained with each other about how to decorate it. The only thing they could agree on was Johnny Depp. So there on one nightstand is a lovely framed eight-by-ten of Johnny, and on the other is a picture I came across while organizing. It's of Baby Lillian and myself sitting on my front step ten years ago. When she saw them both, she laughed and teared up simultaneously. There was simple fullness of joy in that sweet moment, granted by years of exchange. We have history now, and that is just one of the things I love about God—and Lillian.

. . .

Led worship tonight at church. It took me all of seven minutes to make the trip from door to door as opposed to the thirty that it used to.

Being plugged in to that community on a regular basis has been a treat. The hardest steps were the first few times I had to go and get over the initial discomfort of acclimating to a new environment. It's been nearly impossible over the years to stay fully connected to church because I was always away. Now between bringing Lillian to worship and maintaining my role as one of the worship leaders, it's been hard to stay away.

We meet in a tiny chapel downtown. It's a beautiful setting, enhanced by the meaningful touches of the many artistic people in the small congregation. Candles, fresh flowers, a metal sculptured cross, original artwork—it is all so perfect for me, a delight for the senses.

When the service was over, I was approached by an old musician friend I hadn't seen in years. The conversation wound around to the inevitable "So, what are you doing now?" part.

"Mostly I'm just available." I answered. I know it's an awkward response, but I've earned it, and it is the truth that has been indelibly printed on my agenda for my life right now.

I'm always suspicious when others feel obligated to give you their sound-bite résumé in response to a question like that. I am so far away from wanting to impress anyone or to make people feel comfortable with my choices or lax in their own. I know what I know, and I am doing what I am supposed to be doing. I can't help it if it lays out in one sentence with no commas or colons.

Available was a word spoken to me last year when I gave an arts retreat in Colorado. It's a word that used to sound desperate or nebulous to me but now sits like a jewel in my vocabulary.

I went to this retreat to speak and sing to about one hundred people—the "sifted," as my friend Carolyn pointed out to me after one gig, the people who have been through similar refinings and are walking parallel roads to mine. The sifted received what I brought to them with open arms, and I was duly encouraged. After one session, a beautiful elderly man came to me, spontaneously placing his hand on my head in a way that communicated all things protective and merciful. He prayed for me, for my heart, for my calling, and closed with a simple thanks to God for calling me to be "available." It was the word that had eluded me for the better part of this transformation. I couldn't find the correct way to tell people—in a sound bite—the dramatic refocusing that had taken place. How do you explain deconstruction in a way that communicates radical forward movement?

But there, in one small moment, the word leaped out at me as my ultimate duty for this chapter in my life, and I added it to my grid. It answered the volumes of journal entries, such as:

> *After things like this, I wonder where I fit. I wonder what I am supposed to be doing right now—if anything different. Is this what I am to do? Just shift back and forth, keep juggling? Or is there something I didn't get, something I am entirely missing?*

I never considered the versatility as "the calling," the "reasonable service" of worship.[18] It always seemed like a means to a destination. I am certain that for now, it *is* the destination. It's been a growth to see what God highlights, to be brave enough to put myself in situations I am not familiar with. All my normal linear approach to life has been rolled into a ball of twine. The only thing that makes any sense is the living, breathing revelation that is granted to me along the way. It's messy. Not my old *modus operandi*. But it is what I am now. I am at peace with it.

My musician friend obviously was not. There was that awkward pause, coupled with a frozen grin, where he waited for me to fill in the blank. Then, realizing I wouldn't, he immediately offered the comment that comes back most times now, more for the speaker's comfort than for my own: "Oh—well—that's great! So—yeah (vigorous nodding)—great!"

I was rescued from the situation by Lillian, who locked her arm in mine, leaning her head on my shoulder. Children and pets allow you exit in these moments, so with a line I seldom have had the privilege of using, I ended the encounter, leaving him bewildered: "Well, I've got to get going. Tomorrow is a school day, and Lillian has to get up early. See ya."

As I turned, I saw his eyes cut to my ring finger, noticeably bare, and then to Lillian. I could almost read the question as it flashed across his face: "Now how did *that* happen?"

Tell you the truth, I'm not sure myself. I'm just glad it did.

Chapter Thirty-Two

Preserving Sabbath Space

I'm in a new box today, one filled with mementos from my late teens, my first baby steps into adulthood. On a glorified shoestring hung my whistle, a trophy from my years as a lifeguard. How fitting that as an "infant-adult," I chose to guard lives as they enjoyed themselves.

It was a prestigious job to a nineteen-year-old girl because it came at a high physical price. Every year, I was required to re-qualify for the position, and that came by way of rigorous physical tests. But oddly enough, the tests were not centered on saving others; they were predominantly about being able to save yourself—to save yourself when the circumstances are overwhelming, to know when a situation is too dangerous for you to handle alone, to stay afloat for long lengths of time without expending too much energy, to escape from a panicked victim.

It was a metaphor for my life, this whistle. I didn't know it then, but it is shouting at me now. The concept of creating space for regeneration, for energizing, for building up strength—in short, for Sabbath—is biblical, spiritual. And not just Sabbath the "day" but the "attitude." The relaxing into God's unfolding hours as much as possible, constantly reminding yourself that *He* is in control, and *He* is directing; enjoying the freedom that comes from knowing you only have to walk and trust. The retreat to Him that Brother Lawrence so eloquently describes in his little book *The Practice of the Presence of God*,[19] where he speaks about disciplining his mind to return to Christ constantly throughout the day's chores. It's all been key to this growth for me.

When I came back from my first beach retreat, however, my newfound discipline of protecting my Sabbath time caused a stir among my friends. It started with my going to bed earlier.

It's interesting to note the many clandestine ways one can inquire about another's mental health. I'd been asked several times if I was depressed. The questions began at a dinner we had after I returned. In an attempt to put my friends' concerns to rest, I shared the crux of my "retreat." I strategically timed my soliloquy so that just about when the chocolate decadence was placed in the middle of the table, it would be their turn to ask questions. I think I was about one-third into our collective dessert when someone cried foul and I was sentenced to answer without fork in hand.

Extreme jealousy was the overall response to my time at the beach. I didn't know how many people there were who would love to get away from their worlds for a time and "air out."

We discussed that—how people who don't have the ability to unplug for long periods of time manage to do it. How do they find the ways and the space to keep a pulse on their lives, at the very least? And how do they manage the methods of evaluation and discovery? How could someone do what I did without the extended time? Without the ambience?

It's an answer I had to discover for myself because there were to be no more big blocks of "space" for a very long time. I had to make the journey daily—or at least attempt to—in a scaled-down way. For me it has meant getting up at the crack of dawn every day and, thus, going to sleep much earlier than a writer/musician night owl like me ever did before.

As the last of the chocolate decadence disappeared that night, Angie impolitely thrust a fork in my face, using it to punctuate her point.

"There is no *way* that you got up at five or six every day on that vacation!"

"I did. Honest," I said, hand on my heart.

"Well, *I* can't do that, sistuh! Mama needs her sleep," Angie countered.

"Angie, you can do it any time you want. You don't have to do it the same way I do. Just find the time of day where you can concentrate, a place where you can relax for even ten minutes. Do it in little increments. Do it during your smoke breaks," I suggested.

She bit her pinky nail, lips slightly parted, taking care not to disturb her lipstick, which was still fully intact after the three-course meal. While she thought over what I'd said, the vibrations of her jittery leg rippled the tablecloth. "I just don't think I can sit still that long."

I put my fork to my nose, lightly touching the tip. "That's exactly why you need to."

As I organize the whistle in the box, I think of the many times I've let my mornings get crowded with "stuff" since I returned from the beach. Like the "little foxes" in Song of Solomon,[20] the crowding begins almost imperceptibly. A grape here, a meeting there, four grapes there, a commitment that doesn't fit my overall picture. Before I know it, there is nothing left on the vine and I never see it happening because it comes in such small movements. But the small movements culminate and the end result is loss—great loss.

I know better. I have been so disciplined in this area, but my mistake is always in the thought that I don't have to stay on top of the guarding process. I make little exceptions here and there. I accept deadlines and appointments because they seem very "time-sensitive." I tell myself it is only this "one time" or "for a while," and before I know it, all these tiny little adjustments have filled up my rest time—my time for me, my de-stressing time—and the foxes have consumed my peace, my refuge.

The world is always crushing in on this "space." It seemed selfish when I first began to protect it, like the first few times I had to say no to things in order to preserve it. I had the distinct feeling that people were wondering what happened to the "other" me. In fact, I am certain that all over this earth when people decide to change, those around them take note and decide whether or not they agree with the change. And these various judgments about one's changes probably loom in the distance of any desire to change, like phantom walls, hemming us in before we even start.

But ultimately we all have to live in our own skin, don't we? Bear our own pressures? Our joys and pains can be shared to some degree but not entirely—not on the inside where they resonate the loudest. When the sun descends, we must live with ourselves and our decisions. And we must be comfortable in our own skin each day when we wake up.

Knew then what I had to do then and every day since. These baby steps to "no," like "That won't work for me," have been powerful. They have helped me preserve the space that preserves me and serves others.

Chapter Thirty-Three

Sweet Confirmations

Placing the last of the original retreat art pages in its designated drawer, I marveled at how many goals I've been able to accomplish and how sad it would have been had I never taken this journey. I am certain I would not have known all the things I truly wanted to do had I not written them down in these unedited forms. Some have never been accomplished, like combing my hair every day when I get out of bed and having 23 percent body fat. But I do floss daily, sometimes twice.

The sweetest confirmations have come to me in the strangest ways, straight from heaven's throne in some unmistakable cases. I was reminded of that yesterday when I finally filed the last of 2003 in the picture boxes. In the fall of that year, my sister took a series of photos. They were of me in Belgium at a gathering of the European Episcopalian Dioceses.

It had all started innocently enough. An old friend, Father B., asked me to go to this anniversary to sing "Say the Name" at the primary service. Other than a speaking engagement and concert performance, it was a lazy visit. I took my sister, planning to travel on to Paris when we were through.

The gathering culminated in a dinner at Waterloo. The Europeans are quite different in their faith expressions than we are. There are certain cultural norms that the faith culture in America would probably not readily adhere to. One of these concerns alcohol. There, at this dinner, we stood waiting to be seated at a reception. In our culture, it would be presented with pigs-in-a-blanket or shrimp in phyllo or some kind of wholesale frozen special. In Belgium it was locally brewed beer or champagne. My sister was immediately delighted and surprised. "Hey, I could go to a church like this!" she whispered to me. There among the cleric collars and the music of many languages melding together, we visited with bishops and doctorates about everything from *The Simpsons* to Voltaire. It was so refreshing.

The dinner consisted of finely prepared delicacies, more wine, and the recognition of outstanding laypeople within the various dioceses. Relieved to be a guest, I enjoyed the moment, visiting with those around me, eating freely, and enjoying the amenities. The picture my sister took of me is one of total relaxation. I am there, red-faced in my open-collared blue shirt a bit ruffled, lazy smile on my face, with a light sheen of perspiration on my forehead. It was all so lovely—until they gave the final award, which happened to be to someone who, from the lead-in, sounded a lot like me. As each description found words, I found myself scrambling. My lipstick and composure had long since melted away, and all those who were honored before this award fell into the category of prayer warriors and geniuses.

I pleaded silently with my sister across the table from me, "Not me, right? Right??"

Her tight-lipped expression and slight smirk told me all I needed to know. They called my name, and I sloppily got up and walked to the front of the gathering, smiling at Father B.

There are times in life to tuck and roll, and there are times to just come clean. I came clean. As I was handed the European *Lumière du Monde* award for all my humanitarian work over the past decade, I grappled for words. My stunned acceptance speech started with, "I wish I had known this *before* all your European hospitality was poured!" Not that it would have made a difference really, because the most eloquent statements had already been made by ordinary extraordinary people before me.

My acceptance speech centered on one thing Father B. had said as he ramped up to my name. He cited how he had called World Vision and spoken to a higher-up about my work with them. The person who took the call said, "Don't quote me, but I know it is safe to say that about five hundred thousand people are alive today because of Margaret's efforts on our behalf."

Five hundred thousand. It was a number I aspired to and recorded years ago on my first retreat. It was in my list for the ten-year mark. Most important, it was a number known to only myself and God.

Lillian's room has a closet where I have stored most of the awards I've won over the years. They include four Grammy nominations, four Dove awards, several Songwriter of the Year awards, Lifetime Achievement awards, and other miscellaneous ones. None could compare to the knowledge that I helped five hundred thousand people stay alive. I wouldn't have known that it would mean so much if I hadn't made the list.

The subsequent pictures of myself with Father B., the bishop, and the prayer warrior showed my gratitude, my overwhelming fullness of joy, and my disheveled self. In a way, it was perfect. Me enjoying the moment, relaxing into it with no thought of "appearance" or presenting myself as "all together"; Father B., my longtime friend, showing his beautiful support and the sweet freedom of faith; the bishop, whose creative sermon the day before caused children to giggle with delight in the ancient, ornate church; and the prayer warrior, who dwarfed us all because she knew who she was and what she was called to do and did it all without fanfare.

It was the prayer warrior's acceptance of the commission she was given—to continue to pray for all aspects of the church, both local and global, as she had for years with no title or formal call— that will remain with me always. It was simple, her response to the bishop's closing question as he presented the title for her consideration. "Will you accept?" He closed and waited.

"By God's grace, I will," she answered, "and through His grace only."

Amen.

Chapter Thirty-Four

Broken Bread Feeds Many

I have been historically terrible at keeping flowers alive. I can keep a lone goldfish thriving for two years, but even a hearty cactus will meet an untimely death under my care. It had been that way all my life, until one palm tree fought back.

My mom gave it to me twenty years ago. Its original location in the sixties was at Aunt Maureen's house. Aunt Maureen was a mix between Lucille Ball, Phyllis Diller, and naughty vixen. A former chorus line dancer in Chicago, she was gorgeous. Flaming red hair, with nails to match, perfectly applied bright red lipstick and black eyeliner, she and my mom would spend hours trading stories over coffee and cigarettes in Aunt Maureen's mother/daughter tract house. When Maureen smoked, she made it look like the ultimate feminine wile, holding the lit cigarette both loose and firm in her two long manicured fingers, white trails wafting up in twisting curls toward the popcorn ceiling. She pushed the margin with my mom, who was much more earthy and proper. The day my mom took charge of the palm tree showed the scope of her and Maureen's relationship. Maureen's son, Tommy, and I were in the living room watching television when a very young, hip-swinging Elvis Presley came on, singing and mugging for the camera. Aunt Maureen heard it from the kitchen and dashed in, a flash of drama, taut in her bright lilac pantsuit, dragging my mother behind.

"Ha? Ha? See, Peg? What did I tell ya? Look at his . . . " (She mouthed the missing word behind Tommy and me, but looking at the back of Elvis's angular, gyrating silhouette, I filled in the blank myself.)

"Oh my!" my mom exclaimed, covering her mouth the way she would when something was "vulgar."

"Come on, Peg! You know it's bad in all the right ways!" Aunt Maureen cackled in that wet smoker's cough/laugh. "He's beautiful!" she ended, with her flat midwestern accent in full force as she jabbed her cigarette fingers at the console.

"Well, if you say so," my mom said, careful not to give me the impression that such things were allowable in our household. We'd never seen Elvis before.

Aunt Maureen was the wild card of my mom's friends—not related to us in any way but so loved by all that we knew her and the rest of her family as family. She was exciting. She took full advantage of being an "adult" and all the things it allows you to get away with, like cursing and ogling Elvis. We adored her. She was completely herself.

That day, in an effort to take the focus off Elvis, my mom pointed out the poor palm, which at that moment was just a limbless stump in an ornate planter. Poopsie, Maureen's bejeweled German shepherd, had been using it to sharpen his teeth for weeks.

"Take it, Peg," Maureen said, waving dismissively in the direction of the stump. "I can't do a thing with it." She got Tommy to bring it down from the upper floor of the split-level as we left. I remember Maureen's striking figure at the top of the stairs, fresh cigarette completing the picture, Poopsie at her side looking longingly at the stump. "Maybe you can do a miracle," she said to my mom as we headed to our car.

And as it always seemed to be with my mom, she accomplished the miraculous. That palm flourished and threw branches in a three-foot circumference. She gave it to me when she and my father retired and moved south. I barely kept it alive, but by this time, it was used to trauma, so I was safe.

I had it in New York, drove with it in the front seat of my U-Haul truck when I moved to Nashville, lovingly transported it from apartment to apartment, to house. It eventually stopped growing up and began growing only out. In my old house, the span of its branches reached a staggering six-foot circumference, taking up an entire corner of my living room with no sign of stopping. That's when I decided it was root-bound, a term I learned from my mom when I was little. I bought a deeper planter, lined the bottom with rocks for drainage, got the best soil I could find, and replanted it. In the summer, it stayed out on my deck, and in the winter, I planned to bring it in.

It seemed to take the new pot well until the fall. I traveled about one weekend too long, and the plant fell victim to the frost. When I returned one Sunday morning, it still held its branches in a perfect splay, but they were brown and beginning to weaken. All those years, I'd tried to prepare myself for its demise, which would most certainly be a result of something I neglected to do. But there in the chill of my self-fulfilling prophecy, I fought back tears. I'd done okay caring for it up until now. *Why hadn't I just settled for the six-foot shape? Why did I have to repot it? Why didn't I bring it in that weekend before I left?* What I'd done was obviously too drastic, and the plant was weakened.

I trimmed it all back, brought it in, and watered it like I always had. This plant was as old as I was and was one of the few things my mother gave me while she was still able to make decisions like that.

I tried Miracle-Gro, sun, no sun, less water, more water. Nothing.

Finally, I wheeled it out to the garage and gave up. There was a part of me that wanted to toss the dead stump down the hill in my backyard so it could be a part of my soil. In the back of my mind, there was a sick hope that maybe it would find something out there to make it grow again, something that I couldn't give it. But the irreverence of tossing something so precious to the elements didn't seem right. The alternative, throwing it in the garbage, seemed worse. So it stayed, a dry stump in an antique water barrel, for that entire winter. I was sad every time I looked at it, chastising myself for allowing anything to impede me from bringing it in before the frost.

My mother, too, was in a stalemate, parallel with the plant. A myriad of illnesses ushered in by her hip break slowly stole her away from us all. The plant and my mother were on some plane, and I was grieving.

It was early spring, and I was doing the classic Brooklyn thing: sitting on a lawn chair in my garage in Nashville, door up, looking out. My house was filled with community, a family who had long ago adopted me as their own was visiting. I was in the midst of writing for a new project and didn't want to infringe on their leisure time. I typed away for hours, until my neck ached. My friend Heidi came out to check on me.

"Mag, look!" she said, pointing.

I followed her hand, and less than four feet away from me, the stump sat with a tiny half-inch shoot erect on its top.

"I cannot believe it!" I stammered. There, against all odds, with no water or light for months, long ago dead in my mind, was my mother's miracle, confounding us all, ready to start again in a new place. The first shoot was followed by two more. They grew "up" about twelve inches and settled.

My mother worsened. I flew in and out of North Carolina as she fought at home, at the hospital. And one spring night, the call came from my dad that she was passing. It took me exactly forty minutes to grab a bag and get to the airport. Straight from my garden, I ran in my dirt-smudged clothes, twenty-four gates, barefooted for better speed, holding my pants up with one hand and dragging my suitcase in the other. I made the flight and the midnight drive of three hours. When I got there, she was in that final stage of life where every breath is laborious and you drift in and out of consciousness.

This was excruciating to hear and see. There was a moment when I first walked into her bedroom that I thought, *I can't do this. This is more than I can handle.* But I stayed. I prayed. I waited with her. I gave her water and wiped her forehead. I kissed her and told her what a wonderful mother she is and what an extraordinary person she is—not *was*, but *is*. Because I think one of the worst aspects of dying must be the overwhelming thought that you are the only one doing it, that you are in the minority, when the plain truth is that most people who have ever lived are dead. The living on earth are the minority. I said *is* because it *is* her essence, her true being, that I will encounter again when I meet her in the place where the best of us, the Christ in us, are finally home.

There was much more that passed between her and me and my father that night, but those occurrences and blessings are my sacred memories, and to write them here for all the world to see would seem to belittle their significance and their indelible mark on my soul. This would be a time in life that I would say that I was carried, lifted, able to do what no human should ever have to do. I ushered my mom into heaven with a sad joy that only God could balance. My dear friend Gail, who was in the house with her family the day we noticed the new shoot, gave me this precious note after my mom passed.

Maggie, when I lost my mom, the Lord showed me this: that to birth life, there is great pain, but just like when a baby is born, the joy of the baby begins to overcome the pain of delivery and eventually the pain is something you hardly think about. Your mother labored you into this world, and it was painful—to give you life, it was painful. You had the privilege of birthing her into her next world, and it was painful. You had the honor of giving back to her a little bit of what she gave you.

It was true, and it decreased my pain to a bearable level. In those last moments, I was as comforted by what I *didn't* experience as much as I was by what I *did* experience. I did not experience regret for what I didn't do, for how I didn't try, for the moments I didn't share with her. Because I had, been, tried, loved recklessly, kissed her a little too long, held her a bit too tight, and even in her debilitated years made her laugh and reminded her of how wonderful she *is*. Because I knew that God's presence met me there in those moments. That although they were edged in sadness, at their center were delights that far outweighed the threat of tears.

It was important to me to "be" with her. To treasure every belabored "I love you," to acknowledge every gem she tirelessly attempted to give me through the fog of her deterioration. I would not trade a second I had with her, enjoying her, for all the opportunities missed, all the money not deposited, all the no's that left people baffled. None of it and the world itself would turn my head from the mark I have aimed and continually aim for once I discovered what that mark was comprised of.

After her memorial service, I returned to my new home, one I knew she would have loved. In the front, blooming flowers in all colors and sizes met me, and on the back deck, more of the same, along with my mom's happy palm. In a tiny miracle, meant for me, I noticed the stump higher in the pot than it had been since I'd owned it. The sprigs were still the same, but the core, the body of the palm, was thriving, reaching upward like a tree rather than the shrub it had long mimicked. I deem it a picture of my mom, properly planted in her new life, flourishing under God's gaze, healthy and vital again.

It's a daily reminder of all I would have missed—all the moments stuffed with God's provision, God's fullness, my connection to Him and all He is—had I not stopped and gained clarity.

I am certain of what success is now. I am certain that it looks nothing like metal and fabric, chiseled jaws and thighs that don't touch at the top. It is God and all things that welcome Him to be who He is in and through each of us. The most wonderful aspect of it all is that it is there for the taking, there for those who will seek it:

> "Ask and it will be given to you; seek and you will find; knock and the door will be opened to you."[21]

There was a time when that seemed like a catchphrase for all spiritual maladies. It may be, but more so, it's a detailed, effective promise for those of us who are restless, who are weary, who are ready to live life out to its edges in the "fullness of joy." It requires our dangerous deconstruction, our absolute attention, and our willingness to "let go of something" in order to "gain something."

But this is growth, breaking and regenerating. This is strength, being strong enough to be broken. And this is God, taking it all, time and again, and ushering it into the proper place at the proper time.

This is His beautiful truth: Broken bread feeds many.

And that completes the circle.

Convinced

*I will say that if you're alive, you've got to flap your arms
and legs, you've got to jump around a lot, for life is the
very opposite of death, and therefore you must at very
least think noisy and colorfully, or you're not alive.*

—MEL BROOKS

"Yo!" comes the voice over the telephone. "This is your father."
As if I didn't recognize both him and his distinct greeting. "Do
you have the tickets yet?"

We've planned a trip together to Long Island, where we can see
his brother, his old childhood friends, and my two sisters.

"Yes, Dad, and we are on big planes. No worries."

"Great, now *what* do I need to do when I get to the airport?"
And so begins the explanation of things that no longer intimidate
me because they are so familiar but which surely are daunting to the
uninitiated. It's a miracle that he is willing to go at all. The last and
only time he flew on an airplane was to my house in Nashville
about fifteen years ago. As fate—or Beckeritis—would have it, he
was on a propeller plane in a thunderstorm. That was it for him. In
the midst of the turbulent flight, in World War II valiance, he

offered his *MacGyver* acumen to the flight attendant to pass along to the pilot, in case he "might need help." He hasn't been on a plane since and never planned to be.

But all that's changed now. The adjustment to life without Mom, without Peg, has been hard for all of us in unique ways. Driving by a greenhouse makes me choke up. Hearing of someone else's loss makes Dad excuse himself. And Kate fell apart at the DMV after the whole thing happened, although she's not sure whether or not that was grief or just consumer rage. Janie, my other sister, is mentally retarded. I am sure she doesn't understand what the rest of us do: that death is death, and there is no better word for it. *It* just is. Ultimately, it escapes definition, other than the single, stark fact it represents: irrevocable change.

Change has come to both my family and me. I've ushered mine in expectantly for the most part and braced myself for the things there is no adequate preparation for—like grief, which is the Houdini of emotions, escaping all the usual filters and shields, appearing and disappearing all in its own timing.

And yet this change, this profound grief, has brought unexpected color into our lives in so many ways, as evidenced in this trip. We are planning to put my mom's ashes to rest. Although we honored her wishes to be cremated, we did not have full instructions on where to lay them. But we are a resourceful bunch, and in typical Becker fashion, my father concocted the plan. We discussed all the possibilities. The Great South Bay she loved so much? No. She didn't know how to swim, and besides, my dad knew so many people strewn out between Buoy 1 and Buoy 2 that he claimed it was already too crowded. North Carolina, in their tiny creek? No. It was the place where her illnesses set in. Finally, one day he just knew where to take her: to her favorite garden on Long Island.

Not sure if he would be up to traveling when the time came, he resourcefully secured her planter-urn with packing tape, rolled it in bubble wrap until it was three times its original size, put more tape around *that,* placed it in the middle of peanut packing pieces all inside a Coleman cooler, and sent it via UPS to my sister on Long Island (which by the way, we learned later, is against the law). Kate unpacked it all and set Mom out on the kitchen table in her planter. Feeling a bit guilty about the tiny apartment's disarray, she made a new effort at order, certain that if Mom's essence was anywhere near, she would be proud of having raised such a fastidious daughter.

Color flooded in, too, in our chosen method of dispersing Mom's ashes. We decided that we would each choose a receptacle that reminded us of her, cut a hole in the bottom, and discreetly shake her around her favorite tree. (This covertness was just in case we were doing something against some fire code or environmental ordinance, neither of which we have been able to discern, so we can claim ignorance.)

It is color—and *life*—that I hear in my father's voice as I discuss these things with him now that the trip is upon us. He loved his Peg well, even unto death, and the harder part of that love came at the end. I stood witness to what he would allow me to and found a feast in the moments I was granted to bear with both of them in their struggle.

He and I talk more often now, and for longer periods of time. It's part of what my mom left behind. I had seen my coming-up-for-air process as a spontaneous, God-directed discovery—an anomaly that arrived from nowhere and everywhere at the same time. But now I believe that even anomalies have a seed, and judging from the many stories of my mom that were shared with me after her passing, I was merely fertile ground, a finicky African violet that she loved, pruned, and called by name.

I marvel at the parts of God that found expression in her and imprinted themselves on each of us. She calmed my father over the years and grew her children into creative, principled people. She held nothing back if it served the greater good. She stopped her world for strangers and friends alike. She did it all on her own terms, without apology. She broke the rules and lived by a creed that most would assume was lost on a toddler when she passed it on to me, but it was not, because it has stayed with me all these years: "The good Lord gave us only this day, M. Make something of it."

I am trying to, for sure. That means I move slower, do less with more conviction, and push the boundaries harder than I ever have, sometimes to the point of discomfort. But I am *convinced.* And living out conviction can be the best medication there is for a tattered soul. In fact, I believe it can knit tatters into a beautiful quilt of history and meaning that can bring warmth to all who encounter it.

And that's why my bag of choice for our "Release Mom Day" will be a knitting bag, because that's what God did through her— knit people back together, knit beautiful stories into lives, all out of what might have appeared to others as random pieces.

That's what coming up for air has allowed me to attempt as well, in so many areas, both public and private. Perhaps all my shifting can be summed up this way: Instead of thinking about the future, I started living it. Instead of dreaming about what I could do, I began doing it. Instead of waiting for life to happen to me, I happened in it. It's messy. It requires patience and a good sense of humor. It requires a childlike belief in unseen dynamics and forces.

And so, with those challenges ever before me, I move forward into the only day God has given me, offering to make something of all the pieces I can gather, both tattered and refined. I know that God is faithful to complete the tapestry He started. Of that, too, I count myself thoroughly convinced.

Acknowledgments

I would like to acknowledge the following people for their contributions to this work:

Don Pape, my literary agent at Alive Communications, Inc., for his unyielding belief in this story.

Kate Becker, my sister, for the stories, the history, and her quirky input.

Traci Mullins, president of Eclipse Editorial Services and my editor, whose talents brought this work its sheen.

Denise Berry, who edited the very first version of this book and put me on the right road.

Terry Behimer, editorial director at NavPress, for her belief in this work and the opportunity to publish it.

Glenda McNalley, for encouraging me to write it in the first place.

And last but not least, my family, both natural and extended, who have held my arms up for decades now and whose undying support has given me all the things I treasure.

Notes

1 Psalm 16:11 (KJV).

2 Psalm 138:8.

3 Psalm 139:14.

4 Isaiah 53:2.

5 Luke 12:24.

6 Matthew 18:3.

7 Lewis Carroll, *Alice's Adventures in Wonderland Through the Looking-Glass* (Oxford: Oxford University, 1998), 145.

8 See Psalm 68:5-6; Psalm 146:9; Deuteronomy 10:18.

9 See Acts 2:44-47.

10 Jeremiah 1:5.

11 See Luke 10:38-42.

12 Luke 10:41-42.

13 See Luke 7:44-45.

14 See Luke 10:27.

15 Psalm 8:3-4.

16 Numbers 14:27-28,34 (HCSB).

17 See Nehemiah 9:15.

18 See Romans 12:1 (KJV).

19 Brother Lawrence, *The Practice of the Presence of God* (New Kensington, PA: Whitaker, 1982).

20 Song of Solomon 2:15.

21 Luke 11:9.

About the Author

Margaret Becker is an acclaimed writer, speaker, and recording artist who has appeared before over 3 million people. With over 2.7 million records sold to date worldwide and numerous world tours presenting both books and music, she is recognized for her unique approach and inimitable style. She has authored two previous books and contributed to ten more. In addition, her award-winning writings have appeared in more than twenty magazines.

An accomplished speaker, she is currently presenting the material in *Coming Up for Air* at retreats and conferences, both corporate and private. For music, other books, "Coming Up for Air" study guides, and information on how to have Margaret at your event, go to www.maggieb.com or www.comingupforairthebook.com or call 615-3630-2527. To receive Margaret's monthly e-letter, go to maggieb.com.

Further Links and Info

For information on how to have Margaret at your event, call 615-383-2527. Mention Code CUFA315 to receive an additional 10% off the appearance rate.

Join our Web list at www.maggieb.com to receive periodic updates from Margaret. (The list is private and protected.)

To find a Coming Up for Air Getaway in a city near you, go to www.maggieb.com and follow the links to tour dates.

To sponsor a child or learn more about World Vision, go to Maggieb.com and click the link for World Vision.

Related Products

Coming Up for Air: Breathing Lessons—This hands-on companion guide to *Coming Up for Air* is a self-paced journal for personal evaluation and reflection designed to assist readers on their own journey. It also contains helpful links to various partners who specialize in the life areas covered in *Coming Up for Air.*

Music—A new collection of music from Margaret written from the themes represented in *Coming Up for Air.*

Coming Up for Air—Audio version of the book on CD and downloadable formats (on iTunes site also).

For these products, podcasts, free music downloads, and other Margaret Becker products, see Maggieb.com.

TAKE A MENTAL VACATION
WITH A GREAT BOOK!